Major Muslim Nations

Islam in Asia:
Facts and Figures

Major Muslim Nations

Afghanistan

Algeria

Bahrain

Egypt

Indonesia

Iran

Iraq

Islam in Asia:
  Facts and Figures

Islamism and Terrorist
  Groups in Asia

Israel

Jordan

The Kurds

Kuwait

Lebanon

Libya

Malaysia

Middle East:
  Facts and Figures

Morocco

Pakistan

Palestinians

Qatar

Saudi Arabia

Somalia

Sudan

Syria

Tunisia

Turkey

UAE

Yemen

Major Muslim Nations

Islam in Asia: Facts and Figures

Dorothy Kavanaugh

Mason Crest Publishers
Philadelphia

Mason Crest Publishers
370 Reed Road
Broomall, PA 19008
www.masoncrest.com

Copyright © 2010 by Mason Crest Publishers. All rights reserved.
Printed and bound in the Hashemite Kingdom of Jordan.

First printing

1 3 5 7 9 8 6 4 2

Library of Congress Cataloging-in-Publication Data

Kavanaugh, Dorothy, 1969-
  Islam in Asia : facts and figures / Dorothy Kavanaugh.
    p. cm. — (Major Muslim Nations)
  Includes bibliographical references and index.
  ISBN 978-1-4222-1406-0 (hardcover : alk. paper)
  ISBN 978-1-4222-1436-7 (pbk. : alk. paper)
  1. Islam—Asia. I. Title.
  BP63.A1K28 2008
  950.09767—dc22

                                          2008041211

Original ISBN: 1-59084-836-5 (hc)

Table of Contents

Introduction...7
    Harvey Sicherman, the Foreign Policy Research Institute

Islam in Asia: A Brief Overview 13

Cities and Communities 21

Facts and Figures..33

Further Reading...120

Internet Resources..121

Index 122

A Muslim man performs morning prayers in Srinagar, India. Most of the world's approximately 1.3 billion Muslims live in Asia.

Dr. Harvey Sicherman, president and director of the Foreign Policy Research Institute, is the author of such books as *America the Vulnerable: Our Military Problems and How to Fix Them* (2002) and *Palestinian Autonomy, Self-Government and Peace* (1993).

Introduction

by Dr. Harvey Sicherman

America's triumph in the Cold War promised a new burst of peace and prosperity. Indeed, the decade between the demise of the Soviet Union and the destruction of September 11, 2001, seems in retrospect deceptively attractive. Today, of course, we are more fully aware—to our sorrow—of the dangers and troubles no longer just below the surface.

The Muslim identities of most of the terrorists at war with the United States have also provoked great interest in Islam and the role of religion in politics. A truly global religion, Islam's tenets are held by hundreds of millions of people from every ethnic group, scattered across the globe. It is crucial for Americans not to assume that Osama bin Laden's ideas are identical to those of most Muslims, or, for that matter, that most Muslims are Arabs. Also, it is important for Americans to understand the "hot spots" in the Muslim world because many will make an impact on the United States.

A glance at the map establishes the extraordinary coverage of our authors. Every climate and terrain may be found and every form of human society, from the nomads of the Central Asian steppes and Arabian deserts to highly sophisticated cities such as Cairo and Singapore. Economies range from barter systems to stock exchanges, from oil-rich countries to the thriving semi-market powers, such as India, now on the march. Others have built wealth on service and shipping.

The Middle East and Central Asia are heavily armed and turbulent. Pakistan is a nuclear power, Iran threatens to become one, and Israel is assumed to possess a small arsenal. But in other places, such as Afghanistan and the Sudan, the horse and mule remain potent instruments of war. All have a rich history of conflict, domestic and international, old and new.

Governments include dictatorships, democracies, and hybrids without a name; centralized and decentralized administrations; and older patterns of tribal and clan associations. The region is a veritable encyclopedia of political expression.

Although such variety defies easy generalities, it is still possible to make several observations.

First, the regional geopolitics reflect the impact of empires and the struggles of post-imperial independence. While centuries-old history is often invoked, the truth is that the modern Middle East political system dates only from the 1920s, when the Ottoman Empire dissolved in the wake of its defeat by Britain and France in World War I. States such as Algeria, Iraq, Israel, Jordan, Kuwait, Saudi Arabia, Syria, Turkey, and the United Arab Emirates did not exist before 1914—they became independent between 1920 and 1971. Others, such as Egypt and Iran, were dominated by foreign powers until well after World War II. Few of the leaders of these states were happy with the territories they were assigned or the borders, which were often drawn by Europeans. Yet the system has endured despite many efforts to change it.

A similar story may be told in South Asia. The British Raj dissolved into India and Pakistan in 1947. Still further east, Malaysia shares a British experience but Indonesia, a Dutch invention, has its own European heritage. These imperial histories weigh heavily upon the politics of the region.

The second observation concerns economics, demography, and natural resources. These countries offer dramatic geographical contrasts: vast parched deserts and high mountains, some with year-round snow; stone-hard volcanic rifts and lush semi-tropical valleys; extremely dry and extremely wet conditions, sometimes separated by only a few miles; large permanent rivers and wadis, riverbeds dry as a bone until winter rains send torrents of flood from the mountains to the sea.

Although famous historically for its exports of grains, fabrics, and spices, most recently the Muslim regions are known more for a single commodity: oil. Petroleum is unevenly distributed; while it is largely concentrated in the Persian Gulf and Arabian Peninsula, large oil fields can be found in Algeria, Libya, and further east in Indonesia. Natural gas is also abundant in the Gulf, and there are new, potentially lucrative offshore gas fields in the Eastern Mediterranean.

This uneven distribution of wealth has been compounded by demographics. Birth rates are very high, but the countries with the most oil are often lightly populated. Over the last decade, a youth "bulge" has emerged and this, combined with increased urbanization, has strained water supplies, air quality, public sanitation, and health services throughout the Muslim world. How will these young people be educated? Where will they work? A large outward migration, especially to Europe, indicates the lack of opportunity at home.

In the face of these challenges, the traditional state-dominated economic strategies have given way partly to experiments with "privatization" and foreign investment. But economic progress has come slowly, if at all, and most people have yet to benefit from "globalization," although there are pockets of prosperity, high technology (notably in Israel), and valuable natural resources (oil, gas, and minerals). Rising expectations have yet to be met.

A third important observation is the role of religion in the Middle East. Americans, who take separation of church and state for granted, should know that most countries in the region either proclaim their countries to be Muslim or allow a very large role for that religion in public life. (Islamic law, Sharia, permits people to practice Judaism and Christianity in Muslim states but only as *dhimmi*, "protected" but second-class citizens.) Among those with predominantly Muslim populations, Turkey alone describes itself as secular and prohibits avowedly religious parties in the political system. Lebanon was a Christian-dominated state, and Israel continues to be a Jewish state. Even where politics are secular, religion plays an enormous role in culture, daily life, and legislation.

Islam has deeply affected every state and people in these regions. But Islamic practices and groups vary from the well-known Sunni and Shiite groups to energetic Salafi (Wahhabi) and Sufi movements. Over the last 20 years especially, South and Central Asia have become battlegrounds for competing Shiite (Iranian) and Wahhabi (Saudi) doctrines, well financed from abroad and aggressively antagonistic toward non-Muslims and each other. Resistance to the Soviet war in Afghanistan brought these groups battle-tested warriors and organizers responsive to the doctrines made popular by Osama bin Laden and others. This newly significant struggle within Islam, superimposed on an older Muslim history, will shape political and economic destinies throughout the region and beyond.

We hope that these books will enlighten both teacher and student about the critical "hot spots" of the Muslim world. These countries would be important in their own right to Americans; arguably, after 9/11, they became vital to our national security. And the enduring impact of Islam is a crucial factor we must understand. We at the Foreign Policy Research Institute hope these books will illuminate both the facts and the prospects.

A young Afghan boy gives a thumbs-up as he tries on the helmet of U.S. soldier Chris Hughes in a village near Gardez, Afghanistan. The United States invaded Afghanistan in 2001 because of the government's involvement with terrorist groups. Since then, the U.S. and other countries have worked to rebuild the country, which was devastated by decades of war.

1

Islam in Asia: A Brief Overview

When Marco Polo visited Sumatra in 1292, he made a surprising discovery. In the Ferlec kingdom at the northern end of the island, he reported, "many of those who dwell in the seaport towns have been converted to the religion of Mahomet by the Saracen merchants who constantly visit them." Mahomet is better known today as Muhammad, prophet and founder of Islam. "Saracen" was the name by which Westerners referred to Arab peoples. Within a century after Polo's visit, most of Sumatra—which is today part of Indonesia—had converted to Islam.

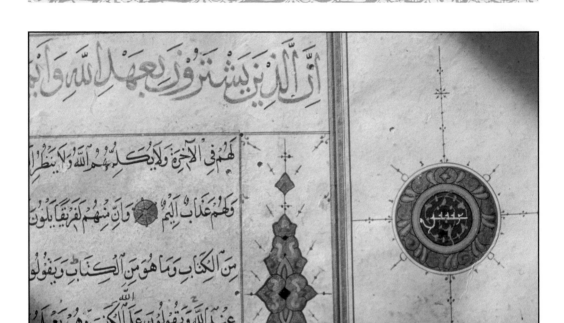

A page from the Qur'an, the holy scriptures of Islam. Muslims believe that Allah's words are recorded in the Qur'an exactly as they were received by Muhammad.

Many Westerners continue to associate Islam primarily with the Middle East. That is a mistaken view. Muslims—whose numbers exceed 1.3 billion worldwide—can be found virtually everywhere on earth. And four countries have larger Muslim populations than Egypt, the largest Arab state. All four of those countries—Indonesia, Pakistan, India, and Bangladesh—are located in Asia. In addition, many other Asian countries have significant Muslim populations.

Historically, Islam as practiced in Asia has differed somewhat from Islam as practiced in the Middle East. In general, Asian Muslims have been less rigid in their beliefs and more tolerant of non-Islamic influences than Arab Muslims. In recent years, however, some Asian countries have seen a marked rise in Islamic fundamentalism—and at least part of this trend can be attributed to the influence of conservative Arab states such as Saudi Arabia.

For these and other reasons, those who wish to understand the place of Islam today cannot simply focus on the Arab world and the Middle East. A well-rounded picture of earth's second-largest religion must also take into account the role of that religion on earth's largest continent.

The Birth of Islam

The beginning of the Islamic era is generally dated to A.D. 622. That was the year the prophet Muhammad (ca. 570–632) and his followers were forced to leave the city of Mecca (in present-day Saudi Arabia) for the oasis town of Yathrib (known today as Medina). Muslims believe that a dozen years earlier, while praying alone in a cave, Muhammad received a revelation from Allah (God). On that occasion, Muhammad was commanded to recite the word of God. Throughout the remainder of his life, Muhammad periodically received more revelations, which he shared with his followers. After the Prophet's death, those revelations were compiled into the Qur'an, Islam's sacred book.

Sometime after the first revelation, Muhammad began preaching Allah's message, the essence of which is that there is only one God and that the righteous must submit to His will. In fact, the word *Muslim* means "one who submits" (to God).

In Mecca, tensions arose between Muhammad's followers and the wealthy and powerful leaders of the city. Meccans were polytheistic, and the Muslim belief in a single God did not sit well with them. This was not merely a theological question: many Meccans profited financially from the pilgrims who flocked to their city to worship the idols at a shrine known as the Kaaba. They stood to lose money if people converted to the Islamic faith.

After years of facing violence and discrimination, the Muslims fled Mecca. But the Meccans mounted several military expeditions against Medina, which the Muslims repelled. The warfare lasted until 630, when

Muhammad and his followers returned to Mecca in triumph. At that time, the majority of Mecca's people converted to Islam.

By 632, when Muhammad died, Islam had spread across the Arabian Peninsula. In the succeeding decades, Muslims would bring their faith to large areas of Africa, Europe, and Asia.

Basic Beliefs of Islam

Part of Islam's appeal lay in its egalitarian message and the simplicity of its practice. Islam did not have a hierarchical structure or a clerical class that mediated between believers and God; instead, it emphasized the believer's direct relationship with God. The essence of the religion is encapsulated in the *shahada*, or profession of faith: "There is no god but Allah, and Muhammad is His messenger." Anyone who accepted this statement, along with a few other basic doctrines, was acknowledged as a good Muslim—regardless of his or her previous religious beliefs, social class, or tribal or ethnic identity.

The *shahada* is the first of the so-called Five Pillars of Islam, the basic obligations of faith and practice for Muslims. The other four are *salat*, *sawm*, *zakat*, and *hajj*. *Salat* is the duty to pray five times daily; Muslims perform these prayers while facing in the direction of Mecca. *Sawm* refers to the requirement to fast between dawn and dusk during the holy month of Ramadan. *Zakat* is the obligation to give a portion of one's income to charity. The *hajj* is the pilgrimage to Mecca, which all Muslims are supposed to try to make at least once in their lifetime, if they are physically and financially able.

Islam Spreads into Asia

Following the death of the prophet Muhammad in 632, Arab Muslim armies emerged from the Arabian Peninsula and began conquering neighboring areas. After defeating forces of the Byzantine Empire in Syria,

A Muslim prays in the Great Mosque at Mecca, Saudi Arabia. Within this vast complex is a square black building called the Kaaba, which is considered the holiest place in Islam. Devout Muslims are expected to make a pilgrimage to Mecca (hajj) at least once during their lifetimes.

Muslim armies moved against the Persian Sassanian Empire. The Sassanian Empire controlled much of the area from Mesopotamia in the west through present-day Iran and Central Asia in the east. But the highly motivated Muslim armies advanced steadily. The Muslims won a string of victories beginning in 637, and many Sassanian soldiers defected to their side. In 651 the Muslims cornered Yazdegerd III, the last Sassanian king, at Merv, in present-day Turkmenistan. The defeat and killing of Yazdegerd marked the end of the Sassanian Empire.

المرآن ثم ارتقما بعد اساطير بلاها ورخارف جلاها وقال اركبوا فيها بسر الله مجرها

ومرساها ثم نقص نفس المعرمين او عباد الله المكرمين وقال لما انا

This drawing from an Arab manuscript shows a *dhow*. These sturdy trading vessels brought Muslims from the Arabian Peninusla into contact with the people of Asia during the eighth and ninth centuries. Islam spread into Asia primarily through trade and missionary work.

That same year, the Muslims conquered Herat (in western Afghanistan) and Balkh (in northern Afghanistan). Afghan territory was soon incorporated into the growing Muslim empire, and over the succeeding centuries Muslims pushed further east, into central Afghanistan and Pakistan. By the middle of the eighth century, the Muslims had advanced into India and to the western frontier of China.

These conquests brought Islam to large areas of Asia. Conversion by no means occurred overnight. But over the course of generations, Islam steadily gained ground. Today it is the predominant religion in all the Central Asian countries, Afghanistan, and Pakistan.

But Islam's spread into Asia was not accomplished solely by the sword. In East and Southeast Asia, particularly, trade and missionary work played a vital role. For centuries, Arab sailors plied the warm waters of the Arabian Sea and the Indian Ocean in their *dhows*. While trading with the peoples of East and Southeast Asia, the Arab Muslims exposed these peoples to the Islamic faith. Gradually, some of the Arabs' trading partners began to adopt their religion.

The gradual and voluntary adoption of Islam in East and Southeast Asia produced several interesting consequences. One of these consequences was the tendency to keep certain pre-Islamic beliefs and practices. Elements of other belief systems indigenous to the region, such as animism, Buddhism, and Hinduism, found their way into the form of Islam that was practiced. Another consequence was that Muslims in East and Southeast Asia were (and continue to be) generally more tolerant of other religious faiths than were Muslims in the Middle East. This relative tolerance is also a hallmark of Muslims from the Central Asian countries of Kazakhstan, Kyrgyzstan, Tajikistan, Turkmenistan, and Uzbekistan.

The Taj Mahal in India is considered an architectural masterpiece. The buildings were constructed as a shrine during the rule of the Muslim Mughal dynasty over India during the 17th century.

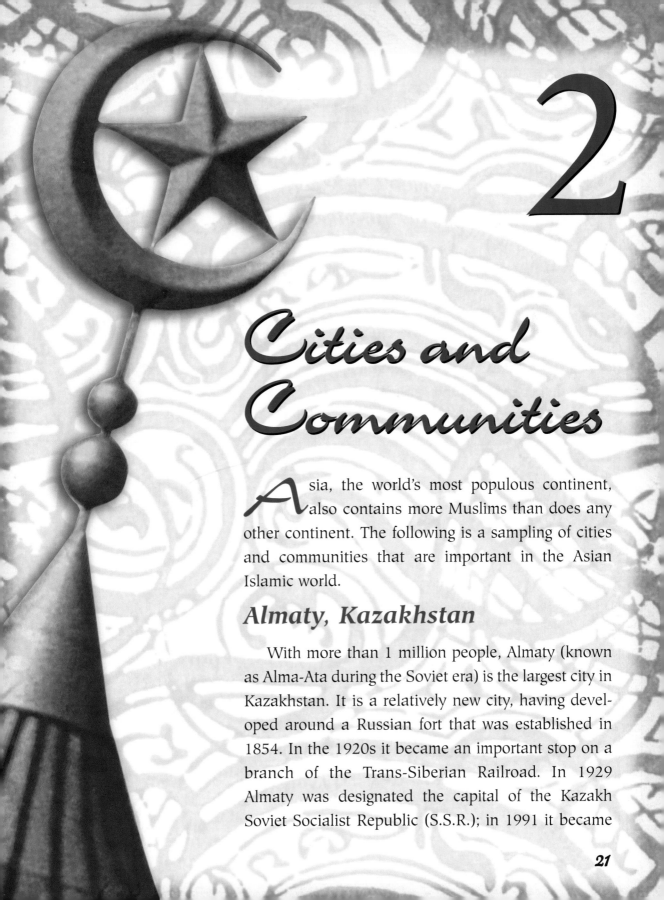

2

Cities and Communities

Asia, the world's most populous continent, also contains more Muslims than does any other continent. The following is a sampling of cities and communities that are important in the Asian Islamic world.

Almaty, Kazakhstan

With more than 1 million people, Almaty (known as Alma-Ata during the Soviet era) is the largest city in Kazakhstan. It is a relatively new city, having developed around a Russian fort that was established in 1854. In the 1920s it became an important stop on a branch of the Trans-Siberian Railroad. In 1929 Almaty was designated the capital of the Kazakh Soviet Socialist Republic (S.S.R.); in 1991 it became the capital of independent Kazakhstan. Although the government has since moved the capital to Astana, Almaty remains Kazakhstan's center of commerce and culture, and it contains the country's largest university.

Ashgabat, Turkmenistan

Turkmenistan's capital and largest city (population 830,000), Ashgabat sits at the foot of the Kopetdag Mountains and at the edge of the Kara Kum Desert. It has been the location of settlements and villages for centuries, but the modern city's origins date to 1881. Today Ashgabat is the business, cultural, and educational center of Turkmenistan. Among the many factories located in the Ashgabat area are ones that produce oil drilling equipment, glass, and processed foods. Ashgabat also has cotton spinning mills, silk factories, and factories that produce the high-quality carpets for which Turkmenistan is renowned. Ashgabat is home to several universities and cultural institutions. It has many green parks, the most famous of which features a large statue of the great Turkmen poet Makhtumkuli.

Baku, Azerbaijan

Once the fifth-largest city in the U.S.S.R., Baku (population 1.2 million) is the administrative, cultural, and industrial center of Azerbaijan. Baku was once the center of the region's oil boom, and its Icheri Sehir ("Inner City") is an intriguing maze of narrow alleys and winding passages dating back to the pre-Russian period. It is surrounded by high fortress walls that nearly extend down to a section of Baku's Caspian shoreline. On the edge of Icheri Sehir stands Baku's best-known landmark, the 11th-century Maiden's Tower, the city's oldest building. In recent years, Icheri Sehir's ancient streets have become Baku's trendiest and most expensive neighborhood, due to foreign companies taking up residence there. The Fountain Square area, with its many shops and restaurants, is Baku's commercial hub. Spreading out from Icheri Sehir and Fountain Square are districts built during Soviet times. They are, essentially, nondescript housing projects where Baku's workforce lives.

Banda Aceh, Indonesia

Banda Aceh is the capital of Sumatra's northernmost province, Aceh. Its population today is about 250,000 people. Banda Aceh has been called the "doorway to Mecca," because it has long been a stop for pilgrims traveling to the holy city. For the past several decades the separatist Free Aceh Movement, which wants political and economic autonomy for their oil- and gas-rich province, has waged a guerrilla war against the Indonesian government. In December 2004, coastal communities in Aceh were hammered by a deadly tsunami, leaving more than 120,000 people dead and more than half a million homeless.

U.S. Navy personnel unload boxes of clean water at a camp for displaced persons in Banda Aceh, a city on the Indonesian island of Sumatra. In December 2004 the island was pounded by an enormous tsunami, which killed more than 120,000 Indonesians and destroyed numerous communities.

Bishkek, Kyrgyzstan

Bishkek (population 794,300) is the capital city of Kyrgyzstan. Before the country became independent in 1991, the city was known by its Russian name, Frunze. Bishkek has a has a long history; it was the site of a Silk Road trading settlement dating back to the eighth century. Bishkek is situated in a valley at the foot of the Tien Shan mountains, and is known for its gardens, green parks, and panoramic views of the mountain peaks. The city is home to several museums, an opera and ballet theater, and Kyrgyz University. Citizens of Bishkek must adapt to extreme weather conditions: summer temperatures can top 100°F, while winter temperatures of –20°F are not uncommon.

Bukhara, Uzbekistan

Uzbekistan's third-largest city, Bukhara (population 250,000), was an important Silk Road city. It rose to prominence under the Persian Empire, and its architecture and culture are of Persian origin. The United Nations Educational, Scientific and Cultural Organization (UNESCO) has included Bukhara's historic center on its list of World Heritage sites. The historic center contains a number of magnificent mosques and Islamic schools. The oldest date to the 13th century, about 100 years before the walls surrounding the historic center were erected.

Dhaka, Bangladesh

Dhaka (population 10 million) is the largest city in Bangladesh and one of the largest cities in the world. It is situated in the geographic center of the country in the delta region of the Ganges and Brahmaputra Rivers. Because of its location on the Buriganga River, the monsoon season brings terrible floods. Dhaka was once the capital of East Pakistan, and became a center for much of the unrest and turmoil that followed the 1947 partition of India. Today the Shahid Minar (Martyrs' Monument) in Dhaka is a symbol of Bengali nationalism, commemorating those who gave their lives for the preservation of the Bengali language.

Dushanbe, Tajikistan

Dushanbe (population 660,000) has been inhabited for thousands of years, but little is known of the city's history until the 16th century, when the territory came under the control of the khanate of Bukhara. The modern city was formed from the consolidation of three smaller towns. It became known for its large and colorful weekly bazaar, an important commercial activity for residents and nearby farmers. A period of rapid growth began in 1929 when Dushanbe became capital of the Tajik S.S.R.; at the time, it had only around 5,000 inhabitants. Today, it is the capital of Tajikistan, and is home to many factories, Tajikistan's largest university, and to the Tajik Academy of Sciences.

Islamabad, Pakistan

Islamabad (population 617,000) is not one of Pakistan's larger cities. It was recently established, in contrast to its twin city, Rawalpindi, which dates back over two centuries. Until 1961, Karachi was the capital of Pakistan; however, the government decided Karachi was too remote to be the capital and construction began on Islamabad, which became the new capital. Unlike most of Pakistan's cities, Islamabad is built on a very open and modern plan. It has parks, shopping centers, and wide streets, most of which run in straight lines. Islamabad's most distinctive attraction is the Shah Faisal Mosque, said to be the largest mosque in the world.

Jakarta, Indonesia

Jakarta (population 9 million) is the capital and largest city in Indonesia. It is located on a flat, low plain on the northwest coast of Java at the mouth of the Liwung River. Once called Batavia, Jakarta today is home to people of many different ethnicities: Sundanese and Javanese from Java, Minangkabau and Bataks from Sumatra, as well as ethnic Madurese, Timorese, Balinese, Chinese, and Europeans. As Indonesia's center of government, politics, media, and business, Jakarta is a key commercial and transportation hub in Southeast Asia.

Jammu and Kashmir, India

The province of Jammu and Kashmir has contributed to more than 50 years of strained relations between India and Pakistan. Most of the people in the province are Muslims, but it became part of India following the 1947 partition of British India. Muslim separatists in Kashmir, supported by the Pakistani government, have requested a chance to determine their future through a plebiscite; they have often resorted to violence to draw international attention to their situation. India and Pakistan went to war over the territory in 1947, 1965, and 1973; during the late 1990s, after both countries had developed and tested nuclear weapons, many experts

Women from Kashmir display a banner asking for peace while marching in a parade in Islamabad, Pakistan, March 2005. The predominantly Muslim province of Jammu and Kashmir has been a cause of tension between India and Pakistan since 1947.

feared tensions over Kashmir would lead to a nuclear exchange in which millions of people would be killed. In 2004 and 2005, Pakistan and India held talks in hopes of resolving the Kashmir situation.

Kabul, Afghanistan

Kabul (population 2.5 million) is Afghanistan's largest city, capital, and economic and cultural center. It sits on both sides of the Kabul River high in a mountain valley near the strategic Kyber Pass. Though it has been destroyed and rebuilt several times, Kabul is one of the world's most ancient cities, founded more than 3,000 years ago. It was an important city in the Mughal Empire, and later was central to the British, Persian, and Russian struggle for control of the Khyber Pass in the 19th century. After 1979, Kabul was the center of the Soviet occupation, and when the Soviets withdrew rival *mujahedin* factions fought over the city. Many sections of Kabul, especially in its western and southern parts, were damaged or destroyed. Today, the city is still rebuilding from the decades of civil war and neglect.

Kashgar, China

Kashgar (population 200,000) was an important city at the foot of the Pamir Mountains on the Silk Road trading route. One of the main attractions of Kashgar is the 500-year-old Id Kah Mosque. It is the largest mosque in China; approximately 100,000 worshippers can attend religious services within its walls at one time. The city is located in western China's Xinjiang province, and most of the inhabitants are Uyghur Muslims. The Uyghurs are a Turkic ethnic group that has lived in China for centuries; in recent decades, some Uyghur groups have waged a campaign to break away and form a separate country, East Turkestan. In response, the Chinese government has cracked down on those it accuses of leading the separatist movement.

Kuala Lumpur, Malaysia

Kuala Lumpur (population 1.3 million) is the largest city in Malaysia. Formerly the administrative center of British Malaya, it became the capital of the Malay Federation in 1957. In 1974, Kuala Lumpur was designated as part of a federal territory within Malaysia, so it is administered separately from Selangor, the state in which it is located. Although Malaysia's legislature and top court are located in Kuala Lumpur, the executive branch of the government was moved to Putrajaya in 1999. The city is a fascinating mix of culture and technology. Within a vast area of 94 square miles (244 sq km) is a variety of colonial buildings and national monuments as well as ethnic markets and modern shopping malls. Towering majestically over the city skyline, the 1,483-foot (452-meter) Petronas Twin Towers is the pride of the nation. The Multimedia Super Corridor (MSC), a government-designated zone devoted to the development of information technology, stretches from Kuala Lumpur to the city's international airport.

Samarkand, Uzbekistan

Samarkand (population 362,300) is arguably the most fascinating city in all of Central Asia. It was founded as a settlement around 3000 B.C., and for much of its early history it flourished as an important city of the Persian Empire. Beginning in the seventh century A.D., the Arabs made Samarkand their principal trading center along the Silk Road, as well as an important center of Islamic thought and learning. The city was destroyed by Genghis Khan and his Mongol armies in 1220, but Timur (Tamerlane), who was born on the outskirts of Samarkand, rebuilt the city in magnificent style and made it the capital of his empire. He encouraged scientists, astronomers, and mathematicians to come to Samarkand, making it the intellectual center of Central Asia. Samarkand later became the

Palm trees and the minaret of a mosque rise in front of office buildings in Kuala Lumpur, the largest city in Malaysia.

During the 14th century, the conqueror Timur Lenk made Samarkand the economic and cultural center of Central Asia. Timur's descendants built the three religious schools that dominate the Registan, sometimes called Central Asia's "noblest square."

seat of an Uzbek khanate, but in 1868 the city fell to the Russians. In the center of Samarkand lies a large square known as the Registan, which means "area of sand." It is surrounded on three sides by remarkable Islamic buildings, the oldest of which dates to the early 15th century. All of these buildings are constructed in the Persian style, with magnificent tile mosaics and sparkling domes. In 2001 Samarkand was designated a World Heritage site by UNESCO.

Tashkent, Uzbekistan

Uzbekistan's capital Tashkent (population 2.1 million) is the largest city in all of Central Asia. For centuries Tashkent was an important stop on the Silk Road, and many of its residents amassed great wealth from the commerce along that important trade route. Much of Tashkent's historic Islamic architecture was destroyed in a major 1966 earthquake. Two structures that survived, however, are a 16th-century Islamic university and the mausoleum of the great Mongol conqueror Timur. Modern Tashkent is a center of education, culture, and business. It boasts Central Asia's largest university, the Tashkent State Economic University, along with more than a dozen other institutes and universities. It is also home to 20 museums, at least nine theaters, and many lovely parks. Tashkent has a modern subway system—the only one in Central Asia—whose terminals are renowned for their attractiveness. Many European and American companies have offices in Tashkent, and the city's industries include airplane manufacturing, chemicals, and silk textiles.

宽 الله اكبر 巷
清真寺

The sign on this mosque is written in both Arabic and Chinese. Although Muslims make up a small percentage of China's population, the Muslim community in China is believed to be about 20 million.

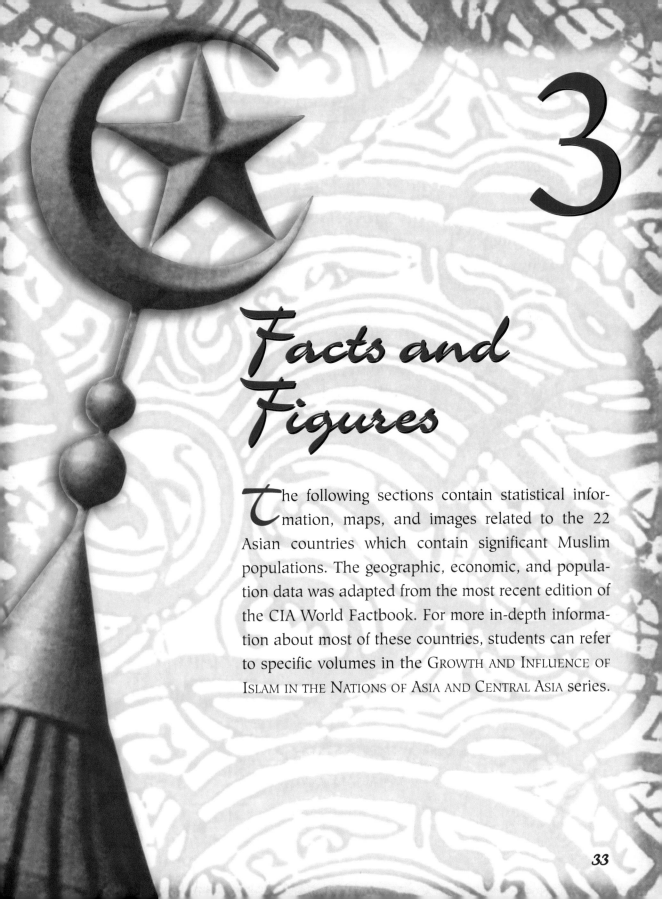

3

Facts and Figures

The following sections contain statistical information, maps, and images related to the 22 Asian countries which contain significant Muslim populations. The geographic, economic, and population data was adapted from the most recent edition of the CIA World Factbook. For more in-depth information about most of these countries, students can refer to specific volumes in the GROWTH AND INFLUENCE OF ISLAM IN THE NATIONS OF ASIA AND CENTRAL ASIA series.

About Afghanistan

The Geography

Location: Southern Asia, north and west of Pakistan, east of Iran
Area: slightly smaller than Texas
    total: 250,000 square miles (647,500 sq km)
    land: 250,000 square miles (647,500 sq km)
    water: 0 square miles
Borders: Pakistan, 1,510 miles (2,430 km); Tajikistan, 749 miles (1,206 km); Iran, 582 miles (936 km); Turkmenistan, 462 miles (744 km); Uzbekistan, 85 miles (137 km); China, 47 miles (76 km)
Climate: arid to semiarid, with cold winters and hot summers
Terrain: mostly rugged mountains, with plains in north and southwest
Elevation extremes:

(continued on next page)

Agriculture is the main source of income for most Afghans. Wheat is one of the major crops, while livestock such as sheep are also raised.

Afghanistan

lowest point: Amu Darya—846 feet (258 meters)
highest point: Nowshak—24,557 feet (7,485 meters)
Natural hazards: damaging earthquakes in the Hindu Kush mountains; flooding; droughts

Sources: CIA World Factbook, 2008; Bloomberg.com.

The Economy

Gross domestic product (GDP)*: $26.29 billion
GDP per capita: $800
Inflation: 13% (2007 est.)
Natural resources: natural gas, petroleum, coal, copper, chromite, talc, barites, sulfur, lead, zinc, iron ore, salt, precious and semiprecious stones
Agriculture (31% of GDP, not including opium): wheat, fruits, nuts, wool, mutton, sheepskins, lambskins (1990 est.)
Industry (26% of GDP, not including opium production): small-scale production of textiles, soap, furniture, shoes, fertilizer, cement; handwoven carpets; natural gas, coal, copper
Services (43% of GDP): government services (including education, health care, and the military), small enterprises

Foreign trade:

Imports—$4.85 billion: capital goods, food, textiles, petroleum products (2007 est.)

Exports—$327 million (not including illicit exports, principally opium): fruits and nuts, handwoven carpets, wool, cotton, hides and pelts, precious and semiprecious gems (2007 est.)

Currency exchange rate: 52.46 Afghanistan afghanis = U.S. $1 (January 2009)

*Gross domestic product (GDP) is the total value of goods and services produced annually (here estimated using the purchasing power parity method).

Sources: CIA World Factbook, 2008; Bloomberg.com

All figures are 2008 estimates unless otherwise noted.

The People

Population: 32,738,376

Ethnic groups: Pashtun, 42%; Tajik, 27%; Hazara, 9%; Uzbek, 9%; Aimak, 4%; Turkmen, 3%; Baloch, 2%; other, 4%

Religions: Sunni Muslim, 80%; Shia Muslim, 19%; other, 1%

Languages: Pashtu (official), 35%; Afghan Persian (Dari), 50%; Turkic languages (primarily Uzbek and Turkmen), 11%; 30 minor languages (primarily Balochi and Pashai), 4%. There is much bilingualism.

Age structure:

0–14 years: 44.6%

15–64 years: 53%

65 years and over: 2.4%

Population growth rate: 2.626%

Birth rate: 45.82 births/1,000 population

Death rate: 19.56 deaths/1,000 population

Infant mortality rate: 154.67 deaths/1,000 live births

Life expectancy at birth:

total population: 44.21 years

male: 44.04 years

female: 44.39 years

Total fertility rate: 6.58 children born/woman

Literacy: 28.1% (2000 est.)

All figures are 2008 estimates unless otherwise indicated.

Source: Adapted from CIA World Factbook, 2008.

About Azerbaijan

The Geography

Location: Southwestern Asia, bordering the Caspian Sea, between Iran and Russia, with a small European portion north of the Caucasus range

Area: (Slightly smaller than Maine)

    Total: 33,428 square miles (86,600 sq km)

    Land: 3,325 square miles (86,100 sq km)

    Water: 193 square miles (500 sq km)

Borders: Armenia (with Azerbaijan—proper) 218 miles (566 km); Armenia (with Nakhichevan enclave) 85 miles (221 km); Georgia 124 miles (322 km); Iran (with Azerbaijan—proper) 167 miles (432 km); Iran (with Azerbaijan-Nakhichevan enclave) 69 miles (179 km); Russia 110 miles (284 km); Turkey 3 miles (9 km)

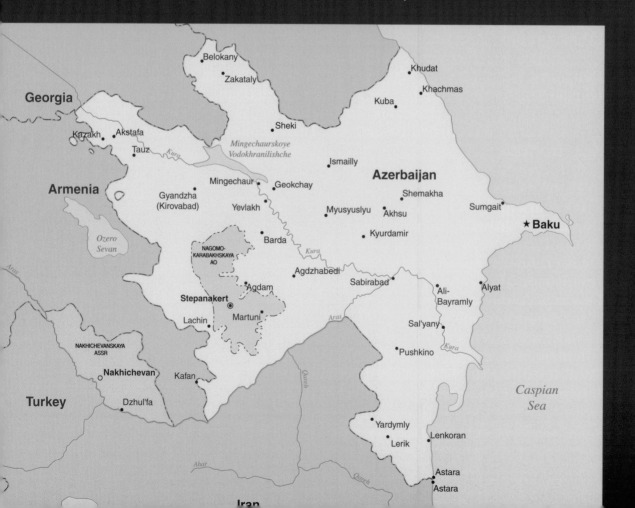

A herdsman guides sheep through the streets of his village in rural Azerbaijan. Agriculture employs two-fifths of all Azerbaijanis.

Climate: Mostly dry and semiarid with subtropical southeast Caspian coast

Terrain: Mountain ranges surrounding a central lowland, fertile southeastern coastal region

Elevation Extremes:

Lowest point: Caspian Sea—90 feet (28 meters) below sea level

Highest point: Mt. Bazarduizi—14,652 feet (4,485 meters)

Natural Hazards: Droughts

Source: Adapted from CIA World Factbook, 2008.

Azerbaijan

The Economy

Gross Domestic Product (GDP): $77.97 billion
GDP per capita: $9,500
Inflation: 21.6%
Natural Resources: petroleum, natural gas, iron ore, zinc, marble, limestone, bauxite
Industry (62.6% of GDP): petroleum and natural gas, petroleum products, oilfield equipment, steel, iron ore, cement, chemicals and petrochemicals, textiles
Agriculture: (6% of GDP): cotton, grain, rice, grapes, fruit, vegetables, tea, tobacco, livestock (cattle, pigs, sheep, goats)
Services: (31.4% of GDP): government, banking, tourism
Foreign Trade:
  Imports: $7.49 billion—machinery and equipment, oil products, foodstuffs, metals, chemicals
  Exports: $38.28 billion—oil and gas (90% of revenue), machinery, cotton, foodstuffs

Currency Exchange Rate: 4,606 Azerbaijani manat = US $1 (January 2009)

*GDP is the total value of goods and services produced in a year.

All figures are 2008 estimates unless otherwise noted.

Source: CIA World Factbook, 2008; Bloomberg.com.

The People

Population: 8,177,717

Ethnic Groups: Azeri 90.6%; Dagestani (Lezghin and other minorities residing in the Greater Caucasus region) 2.2%; Russian 1.8%; Armenian 1.5% (almost all in the Nagorno-Karabakh region); other 3.5% (1999 est.)

Age Structure:
> **0–14 years:** 24.6%
> **15–64 years:** 68.6%
> **65 years and over:** 6.8%

Population Growth Rate: 0.723%

Birth Rate: 17.52 births/1,000 population

Death Rate: 8.32 deaths/1,000 population

Infant Mortality Rate: 56.43 deaths/1,000 live births

Life Expectancy at Birth:
> **Total population:** 66.31 years
> **Males:** 62.2 years
> **Females:** 71 years

Total Fertility Rate: 2.05 children born/woman

Religions: Muslim 93.4%: Russian Orthodox 2.5%; Armenian Orthodox 2.3%; others 1.8% (1995 est.)

Languages: Azeri, Russian, Lezgi, Armenian. Very small minorities speak other languages

Literacy: 98.8% (1999)

All figures are 2008 estimates unless otherwise noted.

Source: Adapted from CIA World Factbook, 2008.

The Geography

Location: Southern Asia, bordering the Bay of Bengal, between Burma and India

Area: (about the size of Wisconsin)

    total: 55,598 square miles (144,000 sq km)

    land: 51,703 square miles (133,910 sq km)

    water: 3,895 square miles (10,090 sq km)

Borders: Burma, 311 miles (193 km); India, 2,518 miles (4,053 km)

Climate: tropical; mild winter (October to March); hot, humid summer (March to June); humid, warm rainy monsoon (June to October)

(continued on next page)

Rickshaws are a major mode of transportation in Bangladesh's cities, and the vibrant paintings that adorn the backs of these vehicles constitute a popular art form.

Bangladesh

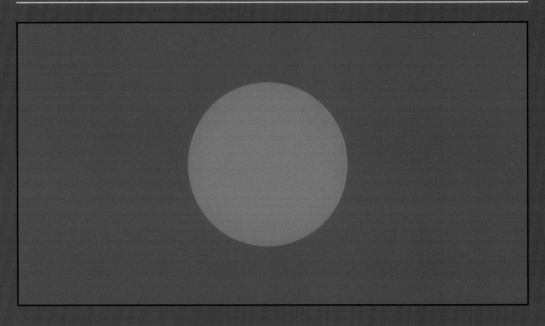

Terrain: mostly flat alluvial plain; hilly in southeast
Elevation extremes:
    lowest point: Indian Ocean, 0 feet
    highest point: Keokradong, 4,035 feet (1,230 meters)
Natural hazards: droughts, cyclones, tornadoes; much of country routinely inundated during monsoon season

Source: Adapted from CIA World Factbook, 2008.

The Economy

Gross domestic product (GDP*): $228.4 billion
GDP per capita: $1,500
Natural resources: natural gas, arable land, timber, coal
Industry (28.6% of GDP): cotton textiles, jute, garments, tea processing, paper newsprint, cement, chemical fertilizer, light engineering, sugar
Agriculture (19.1% of GDP): rice, jute, tea, wheat, sugarcane, potatoes, tobacco, pulses, oilseeds, spices, fruit, beef, milk, poultry
Services (52.3% of GDP): transportation, communications, shipping, tourism

Foreign trade:

   Imports—$20.17 billion: machinery and equipment, chemicals, iron and steel, textiles, foodstuffs, petroleum products, cement

   Exports—$13.97 billion: garments, jute and jute goods, leather, frozen fish and seafood

Currency exchange rate: U.S. $1 = 64.43 Bangladesh takas (January 2009)

*GDP, or gross domestic product, is the total value of goods and services produced in a country annually (here estimated using the purchasing power parity method).

All figures are 2008 estimates unless otherwise noted.

Sources: CIA World Factbook, 2008; Bloomberg.com.

The People

Population: 153,546,896

Ethnic groups: Bengali, 98%; tribal groups, non-Bengali Muslims, 2% (1998 est.)

Languages: Bengali (or Bangala; official), English

Religions: Muslim, 83%; Hindu, 16%; other, 1% (1998)

Age structure:

   0–14 years: 33.4%

   15–64 years: 63.1%

   65 years and over: 3.5%

Population growth rate: 2.08%

Birth rate: 28.86 births/1,000 population

Infant mortality rate: 57.45 deaths/1,000 live births

Death rate: 8 deaths/1,000 population

Life expectancy at birth:

   total population: 63.21 years

   male: 63.14 years

   female: 63.28 years

Total fertility rate: 3.08 children born/woman

Literacy: 43.1% (2003 est.)

All figures are 2008 estimates unless otherwise indicated.

Source: Adapted from CIA World Factbook, 2008.

About Brunei

The Geography

Location: Southeastern Asia, bordering the South China Sea and Malaysia

Area: slightly smaller than Delaware

    total: 2,227 square miles (5,770 sq km)

    land: 2,034 square miles (5,270 sq km)

    water: 193 square miles (500 sq km)

Borders: Malaysia, 147 miles (381 km)

Climate: tropical; hot, humid, rainy

Terrain: flat coastal plain rises to mountains in the east; hilly lowland in the west

Elevation extremes:

    lowest point: South China Sea, 0 feet (0 meters) below sea level

(continued on next page)

Dawn over Kampong Ayer, an unusual community built on stilts above the Brunei River.

Brunei

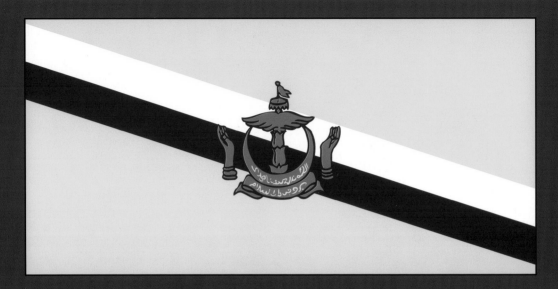

highest point: Bukit Pagon, 6, 070 feet (1,850 meters)
Natural hazards: typhoons, earthquakes, and severe flooding are rare

Source: Adapted from CIA World Factbook, 2008.

The Economy

Gross domestic product (GDP*): $20.65 billion (2002 est.)
GDP per capita: $54,100
Inflation: 0.4% (2007 est.)
Natural resources: petroleum, natural gas, timber
Agriculture (0.9% of GDP): rice, vegetables, fruits, chickens, water
buffalo, cattle, goats, eggs
Industry (71.6% of GDP): petroleum, petroleum refining, liquefied
natural gas, construction
Services (27.5% of GDP): government, education, health, banking
(2005 est.)
Foreign trade:
Imports—$2 billion: machinery and equipment, foodstuffs, chemi-
cals, metals, manufactured goods (2006 est.)
Exports—$6.767 billion: crude oil, natural gas, refined products,
clothing (2006 est.)

Currency exchange rate: 1.4964 Bruneian dollars = U.S. $1 (January 2009)

*GDP, or gross domestic product, is the total value of goods and services produced in a country annually (here estimated using the purchasing power parity method).

All figures are 2008 estimates unless otherwise noted.

Sources: CIA World Factbook, 2008; Bloomberg.com.

The People

Population: 381,371 (2008 est.)
Ethnic groups: Malay 66.3%, Chinese 11.2%, indigenous 3.4%, other 19.1% (2004 est.)
Age structure:
    0–14 years: 27.2%
    15–64 years: 69.6%
    65 years and over: 3.2%
Population growth rate: 1.785%
    Birth rate: 18.39 births/1,000 population (2004 est.)
    Infant mortality rate: 12.69 deaths/1,000 live births
    Death rate: 3.28 deaths/1,000 population
Life expectancy at birth:
    total population: 75.52 years
    males: 73.32 years
    females: 77.83 years (2004 est.)
Total fertility rate: 1.94 children born/woman (2004 est.)
Religions: Muslim (official) 67%, Buddhist 13%, Christian 10%, indigenous beliefs and other 10%
Languages: Malay (official), English, Chinese
Literacy: 92.9% (2001 est.)

All figures are 2008 estimates unless otherwise indicated.

Source: CIA World Factbook, 2008.

About Burma

The Geography

Location: Southeastern Asia, bordering the Andaman Sea and the Bay of Bengal, between Bangladesh and Thailand
Area: slightly smaller than Texas
    total: 261,901 square miles (678,500 sq km)
    land: 253,888 square miles (657,740 sq km)
    water: 8,013 square miles (20,760 sq km)

A Buddhist monk and a Burmese man wearing the traditional *longyi* over his legs walk inside the Shwedagon Pagoda in Yangon, Myanmar.

Borders: Bangladesh, 75 miles (193 km), China, 843 miles (2,185 km), India, 565 miles (1,463 km), Laos, 91 miles (235 km), Thailand, 695 miles (1,800 km)

Climate: tropical monsoon; cloudy, rainy, hot, humid summers (southwest monsoon, June to September); less cloudy, scant rainfall, mild temperatures, lower humidity during winter (northeast monsoon, December to April)

Terrain: central lowlands ringed by steep, rugged highlands

Elevation extremes:

    lowest point: Andaman Sea, 0 feet (0 meters) below sea level

    highest point: Hkakabo Razi 19,295 feet (5,881 meters)

Natural hazards: destructive earthquakes and cyclones; flooding and landslides common during rainy season (June to September); periodic droughts

Source: Adapted from CIA World Factbook, 2008.

Burma

The Economy

Gross domestic product (GDP*): $56.58 billion
GDP per capita: $1,200
Inflation: 27.3%
Natural resources: petroleum, timber, tin, antimony, zinc, copper, tungsten, lead, coal, some marble, limestone, precious stones, natural gas, hydropower
Agriculture (40.9% of GDP): rice, pulses, beans, sesame, groundnuts, sugarcane; hardwood; fish and fish products
Industry (19.7% of GDP): agricultural processing, knit and woven apparel; wood and wood products; copper, tin, tungsten, iron; construction materials; pharmaceuticals; fertilizer; cement, natural gas; gems; clothing
Services (39.3% of GDP): government, education, health, banking
Foreign trade: (not including smuggled products)
  Imports—$3.589 billion: fabric, petroleum products, plastics, machinery, transport equipment, construction materials, crude oil; food products; cement; fertilizer

Exports—$6.149 billion: clothing, gas, wood products, pulses, beans, fish, rice, jade and gems

Currency exchange rate: 6.42 Myanmar Kyats = U.S. $1 (January 2009)

*GDP, or gross domestic product, is the total value of goods and services produced in a country annually (here estimated using the purchasing power parity method).

All figures are 2008 estimates unless otherwise noted.

Sources: CIA World Factbook, 2008; Bloomberg.com.

The People

Population: 47,758,180 (July 2008 est.)

Ethnic groups: Burman 68%, Shan 9%, Karen 7%, Rakhine 4%, Chinese 3%, Indian 2%, Mon 2%, other 5%

Age Structure:
    0–14 years: 25.7%
    15–64 years: 68.9%
    65 years and over: 5.4%

Population growth rate: 0.8%
    Birth rate: 17.23 births/1,000 population (2004 est.)
    Infant mortality rate: 49.12 deaths/1,000 live births
    Death rate: 9.23 deaths/1,000 population

Life expectancy at birth:
    total population: 62.94 years
    males: 60.73 years
    females: 65.28 years (2004 est.)

Total fertility rate: 1.92 children born/woman

Religions: Buddhist 89%, Christian 4%,(Baptist 3%, Roman Catholic 1%), Muslim 4%, animist 1%, other 2%

Languages: Burmese, minority ethnic groups have their own languages

Literacy: 89.9% (2006 est.)

All figures are 2008 estimates unless otherwise indicated.

Source: CIA World Factbook, 2008.

About China

The Geography

Location: Eastern Asia, bordering the East China Sea, Korea Bay, Yellow Sea, and South China Sea, between North Korea and Vietnam

Area: slightly smaller than the U.S.

total: 3,704,427 square miles (9,596,960 sq km)

land: 3,599,994 square miles (9,326,410 sq km)

water: 104,432 square miles (270,550 sq km)

Borders: Afghanistan, 29 miles (76 km), Bhutan, 181 miles (470 km), Burma, 843 miles (2, 185 km) India, 1305 miles (3,380 km), Kazakhstan, 592 miles (1,533 km), North Korea, 547 miles (1,416 km), Kyrgyzstan, 331 miles (858 km), Laos, 163 miles (423 km),

The Niu Jie Mosque in Beijing was built in 997, making it the oldest of the city's more than 65 mosques.

Mongolia, 1,805 miles (4,677 km), Nepal, 477 miles (1,236 km), Pakistan, 202 miles (523 km), Russia (northeast), 1392 miles,(3,605 km), Russia (northwest), 15 miles (40 km), Tajikistan, 160 miles (414 km), Vietnam, 494 miles (1,281 km)

Climate: extremely diverse; tropical in south to subarctic in north

Terrain: mostly mountains, high plateaus, deserts in the west, plains, deltas, and hills in east

Elevation extremes:

    lowest point: Turpan Pendi –505 feet (-154 meters) below sea level

    highest point: Mount Everest 29,035 feet (8,850 meters)

Natural hazards: frequent typhoons (about five per year along southern and eastern coasts); damaging floods; tsunamis; earthquakes; droughts; land subsidence

Source: Adapted from CIA World Factbook, 2008.

China

The Economy

Gross domestic product (GDP*): $7.8 trillion
GDP per capita: $6,100
Inflation: 6%
Natural resources: coal, iron ore, petroleum, natural gas, mercury, tin, tungsten, antimony, manganese, molybdenum, vanadium, magnetite, aluminum, lead, zinc, uranium, hydropower potential (world's largest)
Agriculture (10.6% of GDP): rice, wheat, potatoes, sorghum, peanuts, tea, millet, barley, cotton, oilseed, pork, fish
Industry (49.2% of GDP): iron and steel, coal, machine building, armaments, textiles and apparel, petroleum, cement, chemical fertilizers, footwear, toys, food processing, automobiles, consumer electronics, telecommunications, aluminum, mining and ore processing, locomotives and train cars, ships, aircraft, space launch vehicles, satellites
Services (40.2% of GDP): government, education, health, banking
Foreign trade:
    Imports—$1.156 trillion: electrical machinery, medical equipment, oil and mineral fuels, plastics, chemicals

Exports—$1.465 trillion: machinery and equipment, textiles and clothing, footwear, toys and sporting goods, mineral fuels, iron and steel, metal ores, data processing equipment

Currency exchange rate: 6.838 Chinese Yuan = U.S. $1 (January 2009)

*GDP, or gross domestic product, is the total value of goods and services produced in a country annually (here estimated using the purchasing power parity method).

All figures are 2008 estimates unless otherwise noted. Sources: CIA World Factbook, 2008; Bloomberg.com.

The People

Population: 1,330,044,544 (July 2008 est.)

Ethnic groups: Han Chinese 91.5%, Zhuang, Uyghur, Hui, Yi, Tibetan, Miao, Manchu, Mongol, Buyi, Korean, and other nationalities 8.5%

Age Structure:

0–14 years: 20.1%

15–64 years: 71.99%

65 years and over: 8%

Population growth rate: 0.62%

Birth rate: 13.71 births/1,000 population

Infant mortality rate: 21.16 deaths/1,000 live births

Death rate: 7.03 deaths/1,000 population

Life expectancy at birth:

total population: 73.18 years

males: 71.37 years

females: 75.18 years

Total fertility rate: 1.77 children born/woman

Religions: Daoist (Taoist), Buddhist, Muslim 1%-2%, Christian 3%-4%, officially atheist (2002 est.)

Languages: Standard Chinese or Mandarin (Putonghua, based on the Beijing dialect), Yue (Cantonese), Wu (Shanghaiese), Minbei (Fuzhou), Minnan (Hokkien-Taiwanese), Xiang, Gan, Hakka dialects, minority languages

Literacy: 90.9% (2000 est.)

All figures are 2008 estimates unless otherwise indicated.

Source: CIA World Factbook, 2008.

About India

The Geography

Location: Southern Asia, bordering the Arabian Sea and the Bay of Bengal, between Burma and Pakistan

Area: slightly more than one-third the size of the U.S.

  total: 1,269,010 square miles (3,287,590 sq km)

  land: 1,147,651 square miles (2,973,190 sq km)

  water: 121,358 square miles (314,400 sq km)

Borders: Bangladesh, 1,564 miles (4,053 km), Bhutan, 234 miles (605 km), Burma, 565 miles (1,463 km), China, 1,305 miles (3,380 km), Nepal, 652 miles (1,690 km), Pakistan, 1,124 miles (2,912 km)

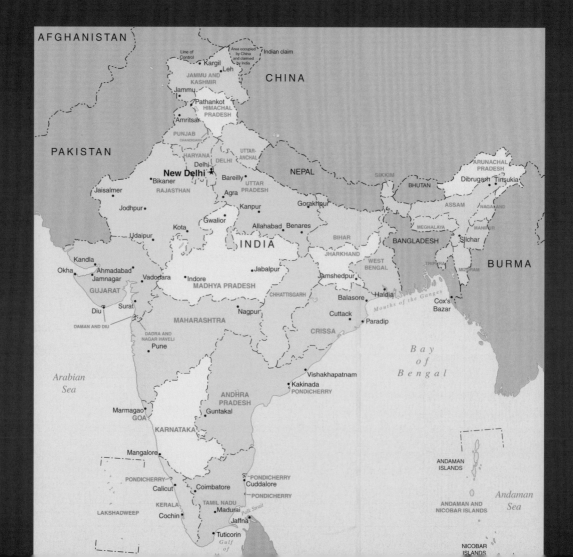

Muslim girls learn their lessons in an Islamic school in Ladakh, India.

Climate: varies from tropical monsoon in south to temperate in north
Terrain: upland plain (Deccan Plateau) in south, flat to rolling plain along the Ganges, deserts in the west, Himalayas in north
Elevation extremes:
    lowest point: Indian Ocean 0 feet (0 meters) below sea level
    highest point: Kanchenjunga 28,209 feet (8,598 meters)
Natural hazards: droughts; flash floods, as well as widespread and destructive flooding from monsoonal rains; severe thunderstorms, earthquakes

Source: Adapted from CIA World Factbook, 2008.

The Economy

Gross domestic product (GDP*): $3.319 trillion
GDP per capita: $2,900
Inflation: 7.8%
Natural resources: coal (fourth-largest reserves in the world), iron ore, manganese, mica, bauxite, titanium ore, chromite, natural gas, diamonds, petroleum, limestone, arable land

India

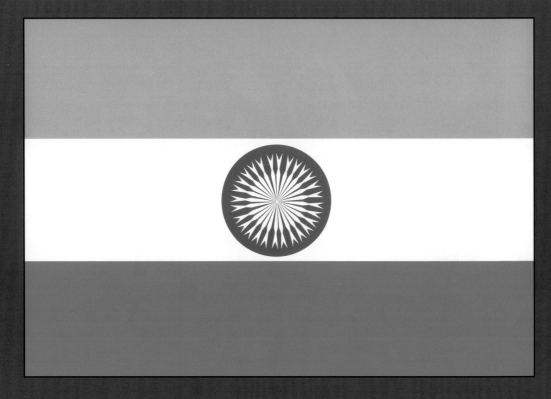

Agriculture (17.2% of GDP): rice, wheat, oilseed, cotton, jute, tea, sugarcane, potatoes; cattle, water buffalo, sheep, goats, poultry; fish

Industry (29.1% of GDP): textiles, chemicals, food processing, steel, transportation equipment, cement, mining, petroleum, machinery, software

Services (53.7% of GDP): government, education, health, banking, tourism

Foreign trade:
    Imports—$287.5 billion: crude oil, machinery, gems, fertilizer, chemicals
    Exports—$175.7 billion: textile goods, gems and jewelry, engineering goods, chemicals, leather manufacturers

Currency exchange rate: 49.11 Indian rupees = U.S. $1 (January 2009)

*GDP, or gross domestic product, is the total value of goods and services produced in a country annually (here estimated using the purchasing power parity method).

All figures are 2008 estimates unless otherwise noted.

Sources: CIA World Factbook, 2008; Bloomberg.com.

The People

Population: 1,147,995,904 (July 2008 est.)
Ethnic groups: Indo-Aryan 72%, Dravidian 25%, Mongoloid and other 3% (2000)
Age Structure:
    0–14 years: 31.5%
    15–64 years: 63.3%
    65 years and over: 5.2%
Population growth rate: 1.578%
    Birth rate: 22.22 births/1,000 population
    Infant mortality rate: 32.31 deaths/1,000 live births
    Death rate: 6.4 deaths/1,000 population
Life expectancy at birth:
    total population: 69.25 years
    males: 66.87 years
    females: 71.89 years
Total fertility rate: 2.76 children born/woman
Religions: Hindu 80.5%, Muslim 13.4%, Christian 2.3%, Sikh 1.9%, other groups including Buddhist, Jain, other 1.9% (2001 est.)
Languages: English enjoys associate status but is the most important language for national, political, and commercial communication; Hindi is the national language and primary tongue of 30% of the people; there are 14 other official languages: Bengali, Telugu, Marathi, Tamil, Urdu, Gujarati, Malayalam, Kannada, Oriya, Punjabi, Assamese, Kashmiri, Sindhi, and Sanskrit; Hindustani is a popular variant of Hindu/Urdu spoken widely throughout northern India but is not an official language
Literacy: 61% (2001 est.)

All figures are 2008 estimates unless otherwise indicated.
Source: CIA World Factbook, 2008.

About Indonesia

The Geography

Location: Southeastern Asia, an archipelago between the Indian Ocean and the Pacific Ocean that straddles the equator

Area: (slightly less than three times the size of Texas)
    total: 740,904 square miles (1,919,440 sq km)
    land: 705,006 square miles (1,826,440 sq km)
    water: 35,898 square miles (93,000 sq km)

Borders: East Timor, 141 miles (228 km); Malaysia, 1,107 miles (1,782 km); Papua New Guinea, 509 miles (820 km)

Indonesia

Climate: tropical overall, but more moderate in highlands
Terrain: mostly coastal lowlands; larger islands have
interior mountains
Elevation extremes:
lowest point: Indian Ocean, 0 feet
highest point: Puncak Jaya, 16,502 feet (5,030 meters)
Natural Hazards: occasional floods, severe droughts, tsunamis, earthquakes, volcanoes, forest fires

Source: Adapted from CIA World Factbook, 2008.

The Economy

Gross domestic product (GDP*): $932.1 billion
Per capita income: $3,900
Inflation: 10.5%
Natural resources: petroleum, natural gas, tin, nickel, timber, bauxite, copper, fertile soils, coal, gold, silver
Industry (45.6% of GDP): petroleum and natural gas, textiles, apparel, footwear, mining, cement, chemical fertilizers, plywood, rubber, food, tourism
Agriculture (13.5% of GDP): rice, cassava (tapioca), peanuts, rubber, cocoa, coffee, palm oil, copra, poultry, beef, pork, eggs
Services (40.8% of GDP): communications, transportation, shipping
Foreign trade:
   Imports: $114.3 billion—machinery and equipment, chemicals, fuels, foodstuffs
   Exports: $141 billion—oil and gas, electrical appliances, plywood,

textiles, rubber

Currency exchange rate: U.S. $1 = 11,325 Indonesian rupiah (January 2009)

*GDP, or gross domestic product, is the total value of goods and services produced in a country annually.

All figures are 2008 estimates unless otherwise noted.

Sources: U.S. Department of State; Bloomberg.com, CIA World Factbook, 2008.

The People

Population: 237,512,352

Ethnic groups: Javanese 40.6%, Sundanese 15%, Madurese 3.3%, Minangkabau 2.7%, Bugis 2.4%, Betani 2.4%, Banten 2%, Banjar 1.7%, other 29.9% (2000 est.)

Age structure:
- **0–14 years:** 28.4%
- **15–64 years:** 65.7%
- **65 years and over:** 5.8%

Population growth rate: 1.175%

Birth rate: 19.24 births/1,000 population

Infant mortality rate: 31.04 deaths/1,000 live births

Death rate: 6.24 deaths/1,000 population

Life expectancy at birth:
- **total population:** 70.46 years
- **male:** 67.98 years
- **female:** 73.07 years

Total fertility rate: 2.34 children born/woman

Religions: Muslim 86.1%, Protestant 5.7%, Roman Catholic 3%, Hindu 1.8%, other (including Buddhist) 3.4% (2000 est.)

Languages: Bahasa Indonesia (official, modified form of Malay); English; Dutch; local dialects, the most widely spoken of which is Javanese

Literacy: 90.4% (2004 est.)

All figures are 2008 estimates unless otherwise noted.

Source: Adapted from CIA World Factbook, 2008.

About Kazakhstan

The Geography

Location: Central Asia, northwest of China; a small portion west of the Ural River in easternmost Europe

Area: (slightly less than four times the size of Texas)
total: 1,049,155 square miles (2,717,300 sq km)
land: 1,030,815 square miles (2,669,800 sq km)
water: 18,340 square miles (47,500 sq km)

Borders: China, 953 miles (1,533 km); Kyrgyzstan, 653 miles (1,051 km); Russia, 4,254 miles (6,846 km); Turkmenistan, 236 miles (379 km); Uzbekistan, 1,369 miles (2,203 km)

Climate: continental, cold winters and hot summers, arid and semiarid

Terrain: extends from the Volga to the Altai Mountains and from the plains in western Siberia to oases and desert in Central Asia

Elevation extremes:
lowest point: Karagiye Depression (Vpadina Kaundy), –433 feet

(continued on next page)

A Soviet Soyuz spacecraft and launch vehicle wait on the launch pad at the Baikonur complex in Kazakhstan. During the 1960s and 1970s, Baikonur was the world's largest space center.

Kazakhstan

(–132 meters)

highest point: Mount Khan-Tengri (or Khan Tangiri Shynygy), 22,950 feet (6,995 meters)

Natural hazards: earthquakes in the south, mudslides around Almaty

Source: Adapted from CIA World Factbook, 2008.

The Economy

Gross Domestic Product (GDP*): $184.3 billion
GDP per capita: $12,000
Inflation: 18.6%
Natural resources: major deposits of petroleum, natural gas, coal, iron ore, manganese, chrome ore, nickel, cobalt, copper, molybdenum, lead, zinc, bauxite, gold, uranium
Industry (39.4% of GDP): oil, coal, iron ore, manganese, chromite, lead, zinc, copper, titanium, bauxite, gold, silver, phosphates, sulfur, iron and steel, tractors and other agricultural machinery, electric motors, construction materials
Agriculture (5.8% of GDP): grain (mostly spring wheat), cotton, livestock

Services (54.7% of GDP): government, financial services, tourism

Foreign trade:

Imports: $37.53 billion—machinery and equipment, metal products, foodstuffs

Exports: $66.57 billion—oil and oil products, ferrous metals, chemicals, machinery, grain, wool, meat, coal

Currency exchange rate (2009): U.S. $1 = 121.425 Kazakh tenges

*GDP is the total value of goods and services produced in a year.

All figures are 2008 estimates unless otherwise noted.

Source: CIA World Factbook, 2008; Bloomberg.com.

The People

Population: 15,340,533

Ethnic groups: Kazakh 53.4%, Russian 30%, Ukrainian 3.7%, Uzbek 2.5%, German 2.4%, Uyghur 1.4%, other 6.6% (1999 census)

Religions: Muslim 47%, Russian Orthodox 44%, Protestant 2%, other 7%

Age structure:

0–14 years: 22.1%

15–64 years: 69.6%

65 years and over: 8.2%

Population growth rate: 0.374%

Birth rate: 16.44 births/1,000 population

Infant mortality rate: 26.56 deaths/1,000 live births

Death rate: 9.39 deaths/1,000 population

Life expectancy at birth:

total population: 67.55 years

male: 62.64 years

female: 73.16 years

Total fertility rate: 1.88 children born/woman

Literacy: 99.5% (1999 est.)

All figures are 2008 estimates unless otherwise noted.

Source: Adapted from CIA World Factbook, 2008.

About Kyrgyzstan

The Geography

Location: Central Asia on China's western border
Area: slightly smaller than South Dakota
    total: 76,600 square miles (198,500 sq km)
    land: 74,600 square miles (191,300 sq km)
    water: 2,808 square miles (7,200 sq km)
Borders: China, 532 miles (858 km); Kazakhstan, 652 miles (1,051 km);
    Tajikistan, 539 miles (870 km); Uzbekistan, 681 miles (1,099 km)
Climate: dry continental to polar in the upper Tian Shan Mountains; sub-
    tropical in the Fergana Valley; temperate in the northern foothills
Terrain: almost completely mountainous
Elevation extremes:
    lowest point: Kara-Daryya, 433 feet (132 meters)
    highest point: Pik Pobedy (Mount Victory), 24,400 feet (7,439
    meters)

Source: Adapted from CIA World Factbook, 2008.

A group of Kyrgyz protesters wave a banner that reads, "Akayev resign" during a March 2005 rally in Bishkek. Protests erupted when the government tried to rig a parliamentary election. The demonstrations ultimately forced Kyrgyzstan's president, Askar Akayev, to flee the country with his family.

The Economy

Gross domestic product (GDP*): $11.66 billion
GDP per capita: $2,200

Kyrgyzstan

Inflation: 22.5%

Natural resources: hydroelectric power; gold and other rare metals; raw energy sources including coal, oil, and natural gas; mineral deposits including mercury, nepheline, bismuth, zinc, and lead

Agriculture (32.4% of GDP): tobacco, cotton, potatoes, vegetables, grapes, fruits and berries, wool, sheep, goats, cattle

Industry (18.6% of GDP): small machinery, textiles, food processing, cement, shoes, sawn logs, refrigerators, furniture, electric motors, gold, rare earth metals

Services (49% of GDP): government, banking, tourism

Foreign trade:

Imports—$3.476 billion: oil and gas, machinery and equipment, chemicals, foodstuffs

Exports—$1.676 billion: cotton, wool, meat, tobacco, gold, mercury, uranium, natural gas, hydropower, machinery, shoes

Currency exchange rate (2009): U.S. $1 = 40.28 Kyrgyzstan soms

*GDP, or gross domestic product, is the total value of goods and services produced in a country annually.

All figures are 2008 estimates unless otherwise noted.

Sources: Bloomberg.com; CIA World Factbook, 2008.

Kyrgyzstan

The People

Population: 5,356,869

Ethnic groups: Kyrgyz 64.9%; Uzbek 13.6%; Russian 12.5%; Dungan 1.1%; Ukrainian 1%; Uyghur 1%; other, 5.7%

Religions: Muslim 75%; Russian Orthodox 20%; other, 5%

Languages: Kyrgyz (official), Russian (official), Uzbek, Dungun, others

Age structure:

   0–14 years: 29.9%

   15–64 years: 64%

   65 years and older: 6.1%

Population growth rate: 1.38%

Birth rate: 23.31 births/1,000 population

Death rate: 6.97 deaths/1,000 population

Infant mortality rate: 32.3 deaths/1,000 live births

Life expectancy at birth:

   total population: 69.12 years

   male: 65.12 years

   female: 73.33 years

Total fertility rate: 2.67 children born/woman

Literacy (age 15 and older who can read and write): 98.7% (1999 est.)

All figures are 2008 estimates unless otherwise noted.

Source: Adapted from CIA World Factbook, 2008.

About Malaysia

The Geography

Location: Southeastern Asia, Malay peninsula and northern one-third of the island of Borneo, bordering Indonesia and the South China Sea, south of Vietnam

Area: (slightly larger than New Mexico)

total: 127,316 square miles (329,750 sq km)

land: 126,853 square miles (328,550 sq km)

water: 463 square miles (1,200 sq km)

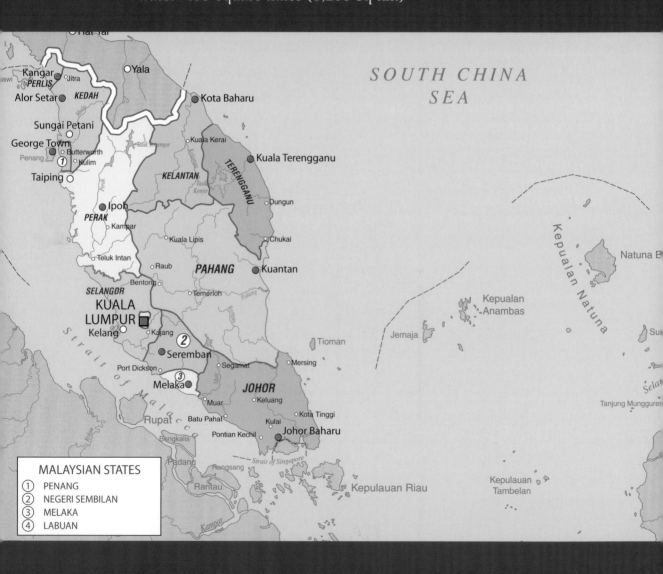

MALAYSIAN STATES
1 PENANG
2 NEGERI SEMBILAN
3 MELAKA
4 LABUAN

Malaysia

Borders: Brunei, 237 miles (381 km); Indonesia, 1,107 miles (1,782 km); Thailand, 314 miles (506 km)

Climate: tropical; annual southwest (April to October) and northeast (October to February) monsoons

Terrain: coastal plains rising to hills and mountains

Elevation extremes:
  lowest point: Indian Ocean, 0 feet
  highest point: Gunung Kinabalu, 13,451 feet (4,100 meters)

Natural hazards: flooding, landslides, forest fires

Source: Adapted from CIA World Factbook, 2008.

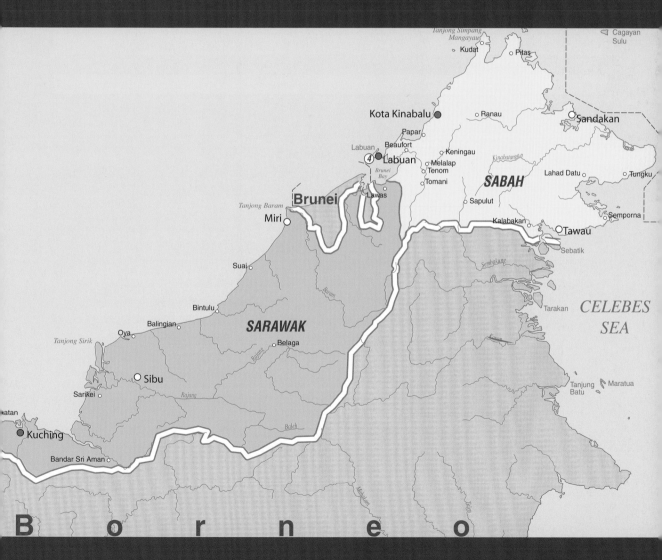

Malaysia

The Economy

Gross Domestic Product (GDP*): $397.5 billion
GDP per capita: $15,700
Inflation: 5.8%
Natural resources: tin, petroleum, timber, copper, iron ore, natural gas, bauxite
Industry (44.6% of GDP): Peninsular Malaysia—rubber and oil palm processing and manufacturing, light manufacturing industry, electronics, tin mining and smelting, logging and processing timber; Sabah—logging, petroleum production; Sarawak—agriculture processing, petroleum production and refining, logging
Agriculture (9.7% of GDP): Peninsular Malaysia—rubber, palm oil, cocoa, rice; Sabah—subsistence crops, rubber, timber, coconuts, rice; Sarawak—rubber, pepper; timber
Services (45.7% of GDP): civil service, public services, utilities, transportation, communications, education and health services, engineering, consulting, architecture, construction, insurance, finance, tourism, hotels, restaurants
Foreign trade:
    Imports—$156.2 billion: electronics, machinery, petroleum prod-

ucts, plastics, vehicles, iron and steel products, chemicals
Exports—$195.7 billion: electronic equipment, petroleum and liquefied natural gas, wood and wood products, palm oil, rubber, textiles, chemicals
Currency exchange rate: U.S. $1 = 3.6 Malaysian ringgits (January 2009)

*GDP, or gross domestic product, is the total value of goods and services produced in a country annually.

All figures are 2008 estimates unless otherwise noted.

Source: CIA World Factbook, 2008; Bloomberg.com

The People

Population: 25,274,132

Ethnic groups: Malay 50.4%, indigenous 11%, Chinese 23.7%, Indian 7.1%, others 7.8% (2004 est.)

Religions: Muslim, Buddhist, Daoist, Hindu, Christian, Sikh; note—in addition, animism is practiced in East Malaysia

Languages: Bahasa Malaysia (official), English, Chinese (Cantonese, Mandarin, and other dialects), Tamil, Telugu, Malayalam, Panjabi, Thai, indigenous languages of East Malaysia

Age structure:
    0–14 years: 31.8%
    15–64 years: 63.3%
    65 years and over: 4.9%

Population growth rate: 1.742%

Birth rate: 22.44 births/1,000 population

Infant mortality rate: 16.39 deaths/1,000 live births

Death rate: 5.02 deaths/1,000 population

Life expectancy at birth:
    total population: 73.03 years
    male: 70.32 years
    female: 75.94 years

Total fertility rate: 2.98 children born/woman

Literacy: 88.7% (2002 est.)

All figures are 2008 estimates unless otherwise indicated.

Source: Adapted from CIA World Factbook, 2008.

About Pakistan

The Geography

Location: South Asia, bordering the Arabian Sea, between India on the east, Iran and Afghanistan on the west, and China in the north
Area: (slightly less than twice the size of California)
total: 310,403 square miles (803,940 sq km)
land: 300,665 square miles (778,720 sq km)

A family takes a camel ride at dusk along Karachi's popular Clifton Beach. Karachi is the largest city in Pakistan, with a population of nearly 10 million.

water: 9,737 square miles (25,220 sq km)

Borders: Afghanistan, 1,510 miles (2,430 km); China, 325 miles (523 km); India, 1,809 miles (2,912 km); Iran, 565 miles (909 km)

Climate: mostly hot, dry desert; moderate in northwest, very cold in north

Terrain: flat Indus plain in east; mountains in north and northwest; Balochistan plateau in west

Elevation extremes:

  lowest point—Indian Ocean, 0 feet

  highest point—K2 (Mount Godwin-Austen), 28,656 feet (8,611 meters)

Natural hazards: frequent earthquakes, occasionally severe especially in north and west; flooding along the Indus after heavy rains (July and August)

Source: Adapted from CIA World Factbook, 2008.

Pakistan

The Economy

Gross domestic product (GDP*): $454.2 billion

GDP per capita: $2,600

Inflation: 20.8%

Natural resources: land, extensive natural gas reserves, limited petroleum, poor quality coal, iron ore, copper, salt, limestone

Agriculture (20.4% of GDP): cotton, wheat, rice, sugarcane, fruits, vegetables, milk, beef, mutton, eggs

Industry (26.6% of GDP): textiles and apparel, food processing, pharmaceuticals, construction materials, paper products, fertilizer, shrimp

Services (53% of GDP): government services, banking, insurance, transportation

Foreign trade:

Exports—$20.62 billion: textiles (garments, bed linen, cotton cloth, and yarn), rice, leather goods, sports goods, chemicals, manufactures, carpets and rugs

Imports—$35.38 billion: petroleum, petroleum products, machinery, plastics, transportation equipment, edible oils, paper and paperboard, iron and steel, tea

Economic Growth Rate: 4.7%

Currency exchange rate (2009): U.S. $1 = 79.85 Pakistani rupees

*GDP is the total value of goods and services produced in a year.

All figures are 2008 estimates unless otherwise noted.

Source: CIA World Factbook, 2008; Bloomberg.com.

The People

Population: 172,800,048

Ethnic groups: Punjabi, Sindhi, Sariaki, Pathan (Pakhtun), Baloch, Muhajir (immigrants from India at the time of partition and their descendants)

Age structure:
  0–14 years: 37.8%
  15–64 years: 58%
  65 years and over: 4.2%

Population growth rate: 1.99%
  Birth rate: 28.35 births/1,000 population
  Infant mortality rate: 66.94 deaths/1,000 live births
  Death rate: 7.85 deaths/1,000 population

Life expectancy at birth:
  total population: 64.13 years
  male: 63.07 years
  female: 65.25 years

Total fertility rate: 3.73 children born/woman

Religions: Muslim 95% (Sunni 75%, Shia 20%), Christian, Hindu, and other 3%

Languages: Punjabi 48%, Sindhi 12%, Siraiki (a Punjabi variant) 10%, Pashtu 8%, Urdu (official) 8%, Balochi 3%, Hindko 2%, Brahui 1%, English (official and lingua franca of Pakistani elite and most government ministries), Burushaski, and other 8%

Literacy: 49.9% (2005 est.)

All figures are 2008 estimates unless otherwise noted.

Source: CIA World Factbook, 2008

About the Philippines

The Geography

Location: Southeastern Asia, archipelago between the Philippine Sea
and the South China Sea, east of Vietnam
Area: slightly larger than Arizona
    total: 115,800 square miles (300,000 sq km)
    land: 115,094 square miles (298,170 sq km)
    water: 706 square miles (1,830 sq km)
Borders: none
Climate: tropical marine; northeast monsoon (November to April);
southwest monsoon (May to October)
Terrain: mostly mountains with narrow to extensive coastal lowlands
Elevation extremes:
    lowest point: Philippine Sea 0 feet (0 meters) below sea level
    highest point: Mount Apo 1,140 feet (2,954 meters)
Natural hazards: astride typhoon belt, usually affected by 15 and
struck by five to six cyclonic storms per year; landslides; active vol-
canoes; destructive earthquakes; tsunamis

Source: Adapted from CIA World Factbook, 2008.

The Economy

Gross domestic product (GDP*): $327.2 billion
GDP per capita: $3,400 (2003 est.)
Inflation: 9.6% (2003 est.)
Natural resources: timber, petroleum, nickel, cobalt, silver, gold, salt,
copper
Agriculture (13.8% of GDP): rice, coconuts, corn, sugarcane,
bananas, pineapples, mangoes, pork, eggs, beef, fish
Industry (31.9% of GDP): electronics assembly, textiles, pharmaceuti-
cals, chemicals, wood products, food processing, petroleum refin-
ing, fishing
Services (54.3% of GDP): government, education, health, banking
Foreign trade:
Imports—$63.42 billion: raw materials, machinery and equipment,

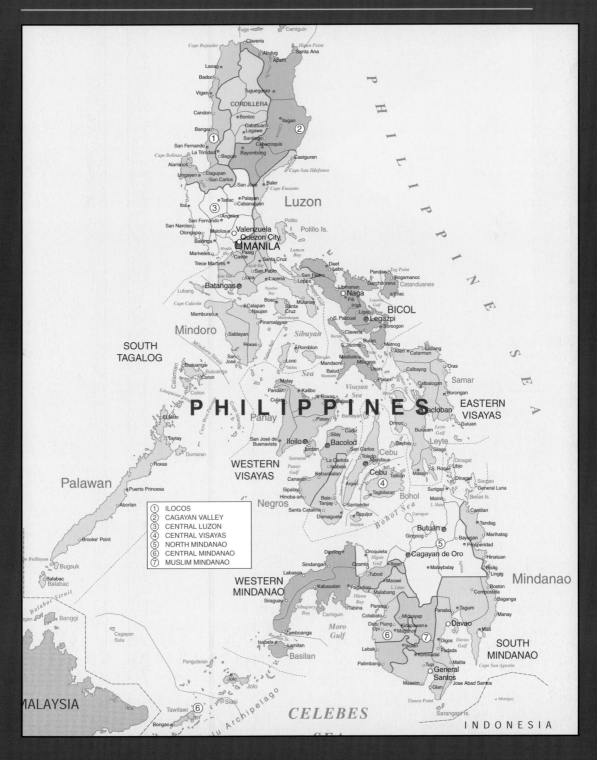

1 ILOCOS
2 CAGAYAN VALLEY
3 CENTRAL LUZON
4 CENTRAL VISAYAS
5 NORTH MINDANAO
6 CENTRAL MINDANAO
7 MUSLIM MINDANAO

fuels, chemicals, electronics, plastic, fabrics, grains

Exports—$50.99 billion: electronic equipment, machinery and transport equipment, garments, coconut products, chemicals, semiconductors, fruit, copper products

Currency exchange rate: 47.319 Philippine pesos = U.S. $1 (2009)

*GDP, or gross domestic product, is the total value of goods and services produced in a country annually (here estimated using the purchasing power parity method).

All figures are 2008 estimates unless otherwise noted.

Sources: CIA World Factbook, 2008; Bloomberg.com.

The People

Population: 96,061,680 (July 2008 est.)

Ethnic groups: Tagalog 28.1%, Cebuano 13.1%, Ilocano 9%, Bisaya/Binisaya 7.6%, Hiligaynon Ilanggo 7.5%, Bikol 6%, Waray 3.4%, other 25.3% (2000 est.)

Age Structure:
    0–14 years: 35.5%
    15–64 years: 60.4%
    65 years and over: 4.1%

Agriculture flourishes in the lush stepped fields of Luzon.

Population growth rate: 1.991%
    Birth rate: 26.42 births/1,000 population
    Infant mortality rate: 21.2 deaths/1,000 live births
    Death rate: 5.15 deaths/1,000 population
Life expectancy at birth:
    total population: 70.8 years
    males: 67.89 years
    females: 73.85 years
Total fertility rate: 3.32 children born/woman
Religions: Roman Catholic 80.9%, other Christian (including Protestant and Evangelical) 11.6%, Muslim 5%, other (including Buddhist) or none, 2.5% (2000 est.)
Languages: two official languages—Filipino (based on Tagalog) and English; eight major dialects—Tagalog, Cebuano, Ilocan, Hiligaynon or Ilonggo, Bicol, Waray, Pampango, Pangasinense
Literacy: 92.6% (2000 est.)

All figures are 2008 estimates unless otherwise indicated.
Source: CIA World Factbook, 2008.

About Russia

The Geography

Location: Northern Asia (the part west of the Urals is included with Europe), bordering the Arctic Ocean, between Europe and the

Russia

- – – – – International Boundary
- – · – · – Republic, Oblast, or Kray Boundary
- – – – – – Autonomous okrug (AOk) or aoutonomous oblast (AO) Boundary

★ National Capital
◉ Oblast Capital

Road
Railroad
Rivers

| 0 | 250 | 500 | 750 Kilometers |
| 0 | 250 | 500 | 750 Miles |

1 KRASNODAR
2 STAVROPOL'
3 ADYGEA
4 KARACHAY-CHERKESSIA
5 KABARDINO-BALKARIA
6 NORTH OSSETIA
7 INGUSHETIA[a]
8 CHECHENIA[a]
9 MORDOVIA
10 CHUVASHIA
11 MARI EL
12 UDMURTIA

a Boundary between Chechenia and Ingushetia has not been established.

An oblast is named only when its name differs from that of its administrative center. Moscow and St. Petersburg are federal cities having oblast-level status.

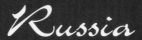

North Pacific Ocean

Area: approximately 1.8 times the size of the U.S.
    total: 6,591,027 square miles (17,075,200 sq km)
    land: 6,560,379 square miles (16,995,800 sq km)
    water: 30,648 square miles (79,400 sq km)

Borders:
Azerbaijan, 110
miles (284 km),
Belarus, 370
miles (959 km),

Sea

Wrangel
Island

• Provideniya

Bering
Sea

Pevek

East Siberian
Sea

CHUKOTKA
(AOk)

• Anadyr'

KORAKIA
(AOk)

U.S.

Kolyma

NORTH
PACIFIC
OCEAN

iksi

KAMCHATKA

YAKUTIA
[SAKHA]

Petropavlovsk-
Kamchatskiy ⊚

Lena

⊙
Magadan

uysk

Yakutsk •

Sea
of
Okhotsk

Okhotsk •

lyuy

Lena

Kuril
Islands

Aldan

nsk

Aldan •

Okha •

Sakhalin
Island

Occupied by
Soviet Union in 1945
Administered by Russia,
claimed by Japan

Amur

KHABAROVSK

Neryungri •

Sovetskaya
Gavan •

Yuzhno-
Sakhalinsk
⊚

• Tynda
Never

AMUR

Berezovyy •

Komsomol'sk •

Urgal •

Khabarovsk •

angarsk

Amur

Birobidzhan •

ATIA

⊙
Blagoveshchensk

AGA
(AGINSKIY
BURYAT
AOk)

PRIMORSKIY
[MARITIME]

al

⊚
Chita

BIROBIJAN
(Yevrey AO)

Sea
of
Japan

Borzya •

Aomori •

Vladivostok •

Khasan •

JAPAN

NGOLIA

CHINA

N. KOREA

Russia

China (southeast) 1,392 miles (3,605 km), China (south) 15 miles (40 km), Estonia, 113 miles (294 km), Finland, 517 miles (1,340 km), Georgia, 279 miles (723 km), Kazakhstan, 2,643 miles (6,846 km), North Korea, 7 miles (19 km), Latvia, 84 miles (271 km), Lithuania (Kaliningrad Oblast) 88 miles (227 km), Mongolia, 1,345 miles (3,485 km), Norway, 76 miles (196 km), Poland (Kaliningrad Oblast) 80 miles (206 km), Ukraine, 608 miles (1,576 km)

Climate: ranges from steppes in the south through humid continental in much of European Russia; subarctic in Siberia to tundra climate in the polar north; winters vary from cool along Black Sea coast to frigid in Siberia; summers vary from warm in the steppes to cool along Arctic coast

Terrain: broad plain with low hills wst of Urals; vast coniferous forest and tundra in Siberia; uplands and mountains along southern border regions

Elevation extremes:
    lowest point: Caspian Sea, -92 feet (-28 meters) below sea level
    highest point: Gora El'brus, 18,481 feet (5,633 meters)

Natural hazards: permafrost over much of Siberia is a major impediment to development; volcanic activity in the Kuril Islands; volcanoes and

earthquakes on the Kamchatka Peninsula; spring floods and sum-
mer/autumn forest fires throughout Siberia and parts of European
Russia

Source: Adapted from CIA World Factbook, 2008.

**A Russian man stands over bodies covered with sheets near a school in Beslan,
Russia. In September 2004, Chechen militants seized control of an elementary
school for three days; when Russian special forces tried to free the hostages inside
the school, more than 200 people were killed. Over the past decade Russia has
battled separatists seeking independence for the predominantly Muslim province
of Chechnya.**

The Economy

Gross domestic product (GDP*): $2.225 trillion
GDP per capita: $15,800
Inflation: 13.9%
Natural resources: timber, petroleum, nickel, cobalt, silver, gold, salt, copper, natural gas, coal
Agriculture (4.1% of GDP): grain, sugar beets, sunflower seed, vegetables, fruits; beef, milk
Industry (41.1% of GDP): complete range of mining and extractive industries producing coal, oil, gas, chemicals and metals; all forms of machine building from rolling mills to high-performance aircraft and space vehicles; shipbuilding; road and rail transportation equipment; communications equipment; electric power generating and transmitting equipment; medical and scientific instruments; consumer durables, textiles, foodstuffs and handicrafts, agricultural machinery
Services (54.8% of GDP): government, education, health, banking (2007 est.)
Foreign trade:
  Imports—$302 billion: machinery and equipment, consumer goods, medicines, meat, sugar, semifinished metal products, vehicles, fruits and nuts, iron and steel
  Exports—$476 billion: petroleum and petroleum products, natural gas, wood and wood products, metals, chemicals, and a wide variety of civilian and military manufacturers
Currency exchange rate: 32.631 Russian rubles = U.S. $1 (2009)

*GDP, or gross domestic product, is the total value of goods and services produced in a country annually (here estimated using the purchasing power parity method).

All figures are 2008 estimates unless otherwise noted.

Sources: CIA World Factbook, 2008; Bloomberg.com.

The People

Population: 140,702,096 (July 2008 est.)

Ethnic groups: Russian 79.8%, Tatar 3.8%, Ukrainian 2%, Chuvash 1.1%, Bashkir 1.2%, other 12.1% (2002 est.)

Age Structure:

    0–14 years: 14.6%

    15–64 years: 71.2%

    65 years and over: 14.1%

Population growth rate: -0.474%

    Birth rate: 11.03 births/1,000 population

    Infant mortality rate: 10.81 deaths/1,000 live births

    Death rate: 16.06 deaths/1,000 population

Life expectancy at birth:

    total population: 65.94 years

    males: 59.19 years

    females: 73.1 years

Total fertility rate: 1.4 children born/woman

Religions: Russian Orthodox 15-20%, Muslim 10-15%, other Christian 2% (2006 est.)

Languages: Russian, other

Literacy: 99.4% (2002 est.)

All figures are 2008 estimates unless otherwise indicated.

Source: CIA World Factbook, 2008.

About Singapore

The Geography

Location: Southeastern Asia, islands between Malaysia and Indonesia
Area: slightly more than 3.5 times the size of Washington, D.C.
    total: 267 square miles (692.7 sq km)
    land: 264 square miles (682.7 sq km)
    water: 4 square miles (10 sq km)
Borders: none
Climate: tropical; hot, humid, rainy; two distinct monsoon seasons –
    Northeastern monsoon from December to March and Southwestern
    Monsoon from June to September; inter-monsoon – frequent after-
    noon and early evening thunderstorms
Terrain: lowland; gently undulating central plateau contains water

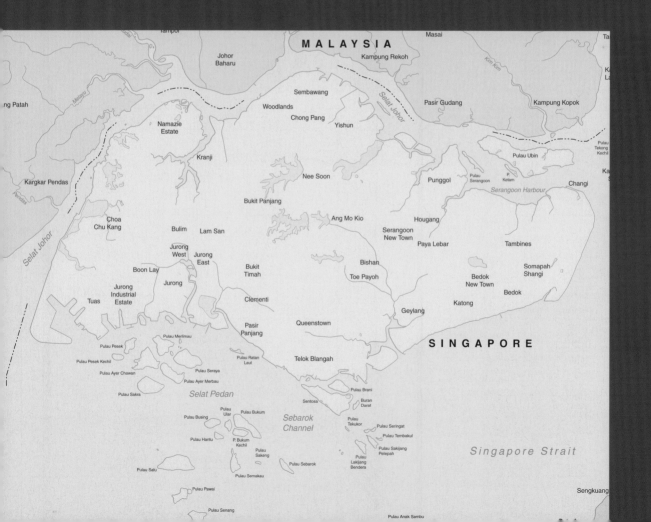

A view of Singapore, taken over Raffles Quay.

catchment area and nature preserve
Elevation extremes:
    lowest point: Singapore Strait 0 feet (0 meters) below sea level
    highest point: Bukit Timah 545 feet (166 meters)
Natural hazards: none

Source: Adapted from CIA World Factbook, 2008.

The Economy

Gross domestic product (GDP*): $244 billion (2008 est.)
GDP per capita: $52,900
Inflation: 6.6%

Natural resources: fish, deepwater ports

Agriculture (negligible% of GDP): rubber, copra, fruit, orchids, vegetables, poultry, eggs, fish, ornamental fish

Industry (33.8% of GDP): electronics, chemicals, financial services, oil drilling equipment, petroleum refining, rubber processing and rubber products, processed food and beverages, ship repair, offshore platform construction, life sciences, entrepot trade

Services (66.2% of GDP): government, education, health, banking (2003 est.)

Foreign trade:

    Imports—$307.6 billion: machinery and equipment, mineral fuels, chemicals, foodstuffs

    Exports—$349.5 billion: machinery and equipment (including electronics), consumer goods, chemicals, mineral fuels

Currency exchange rate: 1.497 Singapore dollars = U.S. $1 (2009)

*GDP, or gross domestic product, is the total value of goods and services produced in a country annually (here estimated using the purchasing power parity method).

All figures are 2008 estimates unless otherwise noted.

Sources: CIA World Factbook, 2008; Bloomberg.com.

Singapore

The People

Population: 4,608,167 (July 2008 est.)
Ethnic groups: Chinese 76.7%, Malay 14%, Indian 7.9%, other 1.4%
Age Structure:
  0–14 years: 14.8%
  15–64 years: 76.5%
  65 years and over: 8.7%
Population growth rate: 1.135%
  Birth rate: 8.99 births/1,000 population
  Infant mortality rate: 2.3 deaths/1,000 live births
  Death rate: 4.53 deaths/1,000 population
Life expectancy at birth:
  total population: 81.89 years
  males: 79.29 years
  females: 84.68 years
Total fertility rate: 1.08 children born/woman
Religions: Buddhist (Chinese), Muslim (Malays), Christian, Hindu,
  Sikh, Taoist, Confucianist
Languages: Mandarin Chinese (official), Malay (official and national),
  Tamil (official), English (official), other Chinese dialects
Literacy: 92.5% (2000 est.)

All figures are 2008 estimates unless otherwise indicated.
Source: CIA World Factbook, 2008.

About Sri Lanka

The Geography

Location: Southern Asia, island in the Indian Ocean, south of India
Area: slightly larger than West Virginia
    total: 25,325 square miles (65,610 sq km)
    land: 24,990 square miles (64,740 sq km)
    water: 336 square miles (870 sq km)
Borders: none
Climate: tropical monsoon; northeast monsoon (December to March); southwest monsoon (June to October)
Terrain: mostly low, flat to rolling plain; mountains in south-central interior
Elevation extremes:
    lowest point: Indian Ocean 0 feet (0 meters) below sea level
    highest point: Pidurutalagala 8,281 feet (2,524 meters)
Natural hazards: occasional cyclones and tornadoes

Source: Adapted from CIA World Factbook, 2008.

The Economy

Gross domestic product (GDP*): $93.32 billion
GDP per capita: $4,400
Inflation: 21.8%
Natural resources: limestone, graphite, mineral sands, gems, phosphates, clay, hydropower
Agriculture (11.7% of GDP): rice, sugarcane, grains, pulses, oilseed, spices, tea, rubber, coconuts; milk, eggs, hides, beef, fish
Industry (29.9% of GDP): rubber processing, tea, coconuts, and other agricultural commodities; clothing, cement, petroleum refining, textiles, tobacco
Services (58.4% of GDP): government, education, health, banking, insurance, telecommunications
Foreign trade:
    Imports—$12.57 billion: textiles, mineral products, petroleum, foodstuffs, machinery and transportation equipment

Sri Lanka

Exports—$9.132 billion: textiles and apparel, tea, spices, fish, rubes, emeralds, diamonds, coconut products, petroleum products

Currency exchange rate: 113.55 Sri Lankan rupees = U.S. $1

*GDP, or gross domestic product, is the total value of goods and services produced in a country annually (here estimated using the purchasing power parity method).

All figures are 2008 estimates unless otherwise noted.

Sources: CIA World Factbook, 2008; Bloomberg.com.

The People

Population: 21,128,772 (July 2008 est.)

Ethnic groups: Sinhalese 73.8%, Moor 7.2%, Indian Tamil 4.6%, Sri Lankan Tamil 3.9%, other and unspecified 10.5% (2001 estimates)

Age Structure:
  0–14 years: 24.1%
  15–64 years: 68%
  65 years and over: 7.9%

Population growth rate: 0.943%
  Birth rate: 16.63 births/1,000 population

Infant mortality rate: 19.01 deaths/1,000 live births

Death rate: 6.07 deaths/1,000 population

Life expectancy at birth:

    total population: 74.97 years

    males: 72.95 years

    females: 77.08 years

Total fertility rate: 2.02 children born/woman

Religions: Buddhist 69.1%, Hindu 7.1%, Christian 6.2%, Muslim 7.6%, other or unspecified 10% (2001)

Languages: Sinhala (official and national language) 74%, Tamil (national language) 18%, other 8%

Literacy: 90.7% (2001 est.)

All figures are 2008 estimates unless otherwise indicated.

A young man casts his net in the shallow water of a lagoon, Sri Lanka.

About Tajikistan

The Geography

Location: Central Asia, west of China

Area: About the size of Wisconsin

    Total: 55,251 square miles (143,100 square kilometers)

    Land: 55,097 square miles (142,700 sq km)

    Water: 154 square miles (400 sq km)

Borders: Total, 2,269 miles (3,651 kilometers); Afghanistan, 749 miles (1,206 km); China, 257 miles (414 km); Kyrgyzstan, 541 miles (870 km); Uzbekistan, 721 miles (1,161 km)

Climate: midlatitude continental, hot summers, mild winters; semiarid to polar in Pamir Mountains

Terrain: Pamir and Alai (Alay) Mountains dominate landscape; western Fergana Valley in north, Kofarnihon and Vakhsh Valleys in south-

(continued on next page)

This grave of a victim of Tajikistan's civil war is located in Qurghonteppa. The violent conflict between Tajikistan's government and an opposition composed of Islamic and secular pro-democracy groups began in 1992. It escalated into a civil war in which approximately 60,000 people were killed before a cease-fire agreement was reached in 1997.

Tajikistan

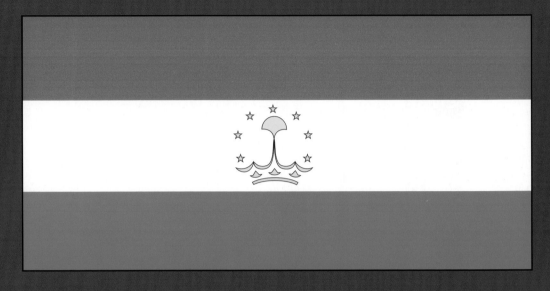

west
Elevation extremes:
    lowest point—Syr Dar'ya (Sirdaryo) 984 feet (300 meters)
    highest point—Qullohi Ismoili Somoni, 24,590 feet (7,495 m)
Natural hazards: Earthquakes and floods

Source: CIA World Factbook, 2008

The Economy

Gross domestic product (GDP*): $13.04 billion
GDP per capita: $1,800
Inflation: 21%
Natural resources: hydropower, some petroleum, uranium, mercury,
    brown coal, lead, zinc, antimony, tungsten, silver, gold
Agriculture (23% of GDP): cotton, grain, fruits, grapes, vegetables;
    cattle, sheep, goats
Industry (29.4% of GDP): aluminum, zinc, lead, chemicals and fertil-
    izers, cement, vegetable oil, metal-cutting machine tools, refrigera-
    tors and freezers
Services (47.6% of GDP): Government, banking, tourism, other
Foreign trade:

Imports—$3.798 billion: electricity, petroleum products, aluminum oxide, machinery and equipment, foodstuffs

Exports—$1.675 billion: aluminum, electricity, cotton, fruits, vegetable oil, textiles

Currency exchange rate: 3.52 Tajikistan somoni = $1 US (2009).

* GDP or gross domestic product is the total value of goods and services produced in a country annually.

All figures are 2008 estimates unless otherwise noted.

Sources: U.S. State Department; CIA World Factbook 2008; Bloomberg.com

The People

Population: 7,211,884

Ethnic Groups: Tajik 79.9%, Uzbek 15.3%, Russian 1.1% Kyrgyz 1.1%, other 2.6% (2000 est.)

Age structure:
   0-14 years: 34.6%
   15-64 years: 61.7%
   65 years and over: 3.7%

Population growth rate: 1.893%

Birth rate: 27.18 births per 1,000 population

Death rate: 6.94 deaths per 1,000 population

Infant mortality rate: 42.31 deaths per 1,000 live births

Life expectancy:
   Overall: 64.97 years
   Male: 61.95 years
   Female: 68.15 years

Fertility rate: 3.04 children born per woman

Literacy: 99.5% (2000 est.)

All figures are 2008 estimates unless otherwise noted.

Source: CIA World Factbook 2008.

About Thailand

The Geography

Location: Southeastern Asia, bordering the Andaman Sea and the Gulf of Thailand, southeast of Burma

Area: slightly more than twice the size of Wyoming
    total: 198,404 square miles (514,000 sq km)
    land: 197,543 square miles (511,770 sq km)
    water: 861 square miles (2,230 sq km)

Borders: Burma, 695 miles (1,800 km), Cambodia, 310 miles (803 km), Laos, 677 miles (1,754 km), Malaysia, 195 miles (506 km)

Climate: tropical; rainy, warm, cloudy southwest monsoon (mid-May to September); dry, cool northeast monsoon (November to mid-March); southern isthmus always hot and humid

Terrain: central plain; Khorat Plateau in the east; mountains elsewhere

Elevation extremes:
    lowest point: Gulf of Thailand 0 feet (0 meters) below sea level
    highest point: Doi Inthanon 8,451 feet (2,576 meters)

Natural hazards: land subsidence in Bangkok area resulting from the depletion of the water table; droughts

Source: Adapted from CIA World Factbook, 2008.

The Economy

Gross domestic product (GDP*): $570.1 billion

GDP per capita: $8,700

Inflation: 5.8%

Natural resources: tin, rubber, natural gas, tungsten, tantalum, timber, lead, fish, gypsum, lignite, fluorite, arable land

Agriculture (11.4% of GDP): rice, cassava (tapioca), rubber, corn, sugarcane, coconuts, soybeans, fish

Industry (44.5% of GDP): tourism, textiles and garments, agricultural processing, beverages, tobacco, cement, light manufacturing such as jewelry, electric appliances and components, computers and parts, integrated circuits, furniture, plastics, world's second-largest tungsten producer, and third-largest tin producer

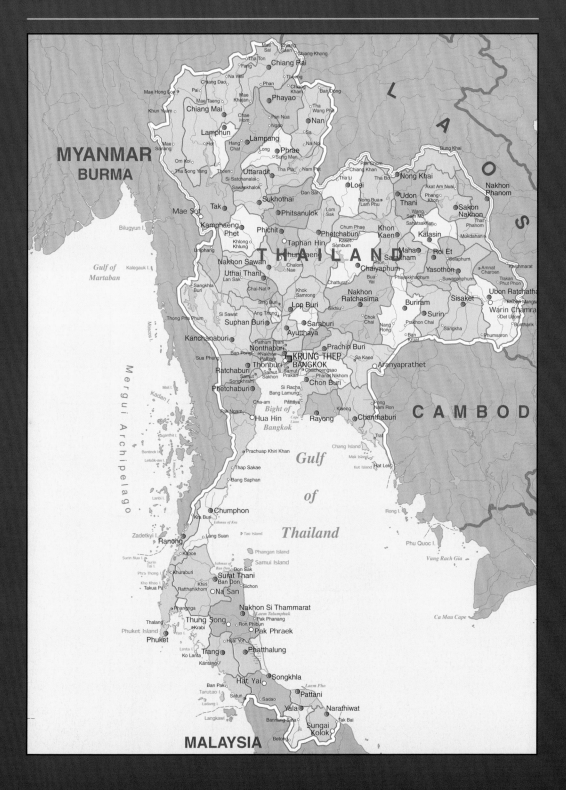

Services (44.1% of GDP): government, education, health, banking
Foreign trade:
   Imports—$159.1 billion: capital goods, intermediate goods and raw materials, consumer goods, fuels
   Exports—$174.9 billion: computers, office machine parts, transistors, rubber, vehicles (cars and trucks), plastic, seafood, rice, fish, clothing, jewelry, textiles
Currency exchange rate: 34.89 Thai baht = U.S. $1 (2009)

*GDP, or gross domestic product, is the total value of goods and services produced in a country annually (here estimated using the purchasing power parity method).

All figures are 2008 estimates unless otherwise noted.

Sources: CIA World Factbook, 2008; Bloomberg.com.

The People

Population: 65,493,296 (July 2008 est.)

Thailand

Ethnic groups: Thai 75%, Chinese 14%, other 11%

Age Structure:

0–14 years: 21.2%

15–64 years: 70.3%

65 years and over: 8.5%

Population growth rate: 0.64%

Birth rate: 13.57 births/1,000 population

Infant mortality rate: 18.23 deaths/1,000 live births

Death rate: 7.17 deaths/1,000 population

Life expectancy at birth:

total population: 72.83 years

males: 70.51 years

females: 75.27 years

Total fertility rate: 1.64 children born/woman

Religions: Buddhist 94.6%, Muslim 4.6%, Christianity 0.7%, other 0.1% (2000 est.)

Languages: Thai, English (secondary language of the elite), ethnic and regional dialects

Literacy: 92.6% (2000 est.)

All figures are 2008 estimates unless otherwise indicated.

Source: CIA World Factbook, 2008.

Thai Muslim girls line up at an Islamic elementary school in Laem Pho.

About Turkmenistan

The Geography

Location: Central Asia, bordering the Caspian Sea, between Iran and Afghanistan

Area: (slightly larger than California)

total: 195,240 square miles (488,100 sq km)

land: 195,240 square miles (488,100 sq km)

water: negligible

Borders: Caspian Sea, 1,096 miles (1,768 km); Uzbekistan, 1,005 miles (1,621 km); Iran, 615 miles (992 km); Afghanistan, 461 miles (744 km); Kazakhstan, 235 miles (379 km)

Cotton remains the most important crop in Turkmenistan, although in recent years the government has attempted to diversify the agriculture sector of the economy.

Climate: subtropical desert

Terrain: flat-to-rolling sandy desert with dunes rising to mountains in the south; low mountains along border with Iran; borders Caspian Sea in west

Elevation extremes:
lowest point: Vpadina Akchanaya depression, –270 feet (–81 meters)
highest point: Gora Ayribaba, 10,356 feet (3,139 meters)

Natural hazards: earthquakes, drought, sandstorms

Source: Adapted from CIA World Factbook, 2008.

Turkmenistan

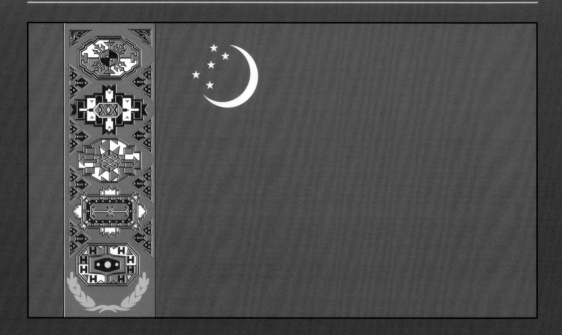

The Economy

Gross Domestic Product (GDP*): $30.19 billion
GDP per capita: $5,800
Inflation: 18%
Natural Resources: petroleum, natural gas, coal, sulfur, salt
Agriculture (10.7% of GDP): cotton, grain, livestock
Industry (38.8% of GDP): natural gas, oil, petroleum products, textiles, food processing
Services (50.4% of GDP): government services (including education, health care, and the military), banking
Foreign Trade:
  Imports: $5.291 billion—machinery and equipment, foodstuffs, chemicals
  Exports: $9.887 billion—gas, oil, cotton fiber, textiles, petrochemicals
Currency Exchange Rate (2009): U.S. $1= 14,250 Turkmenistani manats

*GDP, or gross domestic product, is the total value of goods and services produced in a country annually.

All figures are 2008 estimates unless otherwise noted.

Source: CIA World Factbook, 2008.

The People

Population: 5,179,571

Ethnic groups: Turkmen 85%, Uzbek 5%, Russian 4%, other 6% (2003)

Religions: Muslim, 89%; Eastern Orthodox, 9%; other or unknown, 2%

Languages: Turkmen 72%, Russian 12%, Uzbek 9%, other 7%

Age structure:

    0–14 years: 34.2%

    15–64 years: 61.5%

    65 years and over: 4.3%

Population growth rate: 1.596%

Birth rate: 25.07 births/1,000 population

Death rate: 6.11 deaths/1,000 population

Infant mortality rate: 51.81 deaths/1,000 live births

Life expectancy at birth:

    total population: 68.6 years

    males: 65.53 years

    females: 71.82 years

Total fertility rate: 3.07 children born/woman

Literacy rate: 98.8% (2003 estimate)

All figures are 2008 estimates unless otherwise indicated.

Source: Adapted from CIA World Factbook, 2008.

About Uzbekistan

The Geography

Location: Central Asia, north of Afghanistan
Area: slightly larger than California
    total: 174,486 square miles (447,400 sq km)
    land: 165,906 square miles (425,400 sq km)
    water: 8,580 square miles (22,000 sq km)
Borders: Afghanistan, 85 miles (137 km); Kazakhstan, 1,366 miles (2,203 km); Kyrgyzstan, 681 miles (1,099 km); Tajikistan, 720 miles (1,161 km); Turkmenistan, 1,005 miles (1,621 km)
Climate: mostly midlatitude desert, with long, hot summers and mild winters; semiarid in eastern grasslands
Terrain: mostly flat-to-rolling sandy desert with dunes; broad, flat,

(continued on page 114)

Throughout Uzbekistan, the old and the new stand side by side. In this view of Tashkent, a modern hotel can be seen on the left, with the 16th-century Kukeldash Madrassa at right.

Uzbekistan

intensely irrigated river valleys along course of Amu Dar'ya, Syr Dar'ya, and Zarafshon; Fergana Valley in east surrounded by mountainous Tajikistan and Kyrgyzstan; shrinking Aral Sea in west

Elevation extremes:
   lowest point: Sariqarnish Kuli, 39 feet (12 meters) below sea level
   highest point: Adelunga Toghi, 14,107 feet (4,301 meters)
Natural hazards: occasional earthquakes

Source: Adapted from CIA World Factbook, 2008.

The Economy

Gross domestic product (GDP*): $72.76 billion
GDP per capita: $2,700
Inflation: 13.5% (official rate; disputed)
Natural resources: natural gas, petroleum, coal, gold, uranium, silver, copper, lead, zinc, tungsten, molybdenum
Agriculture (28.2% of GDP): cotton, vegetables, fruits, grains, livestock
Industry (33.9% of GDP): textiles, food processing, machine building, metallurgy, natural gas, chemicals
Services (37.9% of GDP): government, education, health, banking
Foreign trade:

Imports—$6.5 billion: machinery and equipment, foodstuffs, chemicals, metals

Exports—$9.96 billion: cotton, gold, energy products, mineral fertilizers, ferrous metals, textiles, food products, automobiles, machinery

Currency exchange rate: 1,398.37 Uzbekistan sums = U.S. $1 (January 2009)

*GDP, or gross domestic product, is the total value of goods and services produced in a country annually (here estimated using the purchasing power parity method).

All figures are 2008 estimates unless otherwise noted.

Sources: CIA World Factbook, 2008; Bloomberg.com.

The People

Population: 27,345,026

Ethnic groups: Uzbek, 80%; Russian, 5.5%; Tajik, 5%; Kazakh, 3%; Karakalpak, 2.5%; Tatar, 1.5%; other, 2.5% (1996 est.)

Age structure:

0–14 years: 29%

15–64 years: 66%

65 years and over: 5%

Population growth rate: 0.965%

Birth rate: 17.99 births/1,000 population

Infant mortality rate: 24.23 deaths/1,000 live births

Death rate: 5.3 deaths/1,000 population

Life expectancy at birth:

total population: 71.69 years

males: 68.89 years

females: 74.87 years

Total fertility rate: 2.01 children born/woman

Religions: Muslim, 88% (mostly Sunnis); Eastern Orthodox, 9%; other, 3%

Languages: Uzbek, 74.3%; Russian, 14.2%; Tajik, 4.4%; other, 7.1%

Literacy: 99.3% (2003 est.)

All figures are 2008 estimates unless otherwise indicated.

Source: CIA World Factbook, 2008.

About Vietnam

The Geography

Location: Southeastern Asia, bordering the Gulf of Thailand, Gulf of Tonkin, and South China Sea, alongside China, Laos, and Cambodia

Area: slightly larger than New Mexico
total: 127,210 square miles (329,560 sq km)
land: 125,589 square miles (325,360 sq km)
water: 1,621 square miles (4,200 sq km)

Borders: Cambodia, 474 miles (1,228 km), China, 494 miles (1,281 km), Laos, 822 miles (2,130 km)

Climate: tropical in south; monsoonal in north with hot, rainy season (mid-May to mid-September) and warm, dry season (mid-October to mid-March)

Terrain: low, flat delta in south and north; central highlands; hilly, mountainous in far north and northwest

Elevation extremes:
lowest point: South China Sea 0 feet (0 meters) below sea level
highest point: Fan Si Pan 10,315 feet (3,114 meters)
Natural hazards: occasional typhoons (May to January) with extensive flooding, especially in the Mekong River delta

Source: Adapted from CIA World Factbook, 2008.

The Economy

Gross domestic product (GDP*): $246.6 billion
GDP per capita: $2,900
Inflation: 24.5%
Natural resources: phosphates, coal, manganese, bauxite, chromate, offshore oil and gas deposits, forests, hydropower
Agriculture (19% of GDP): paddy rice, corn, potatotes, rubber, soybeans, coffee, tea, bananas, sugar; poultry, pigs, fish
Industry (42.7% of GDP): food processing, garments, shoes, machine-building, mining, cement, chemical fertilizer, glass, tires, oil, coal, steel, paper
Services (38.4% of GDP): government, education, health, banking

1. LAI CHAU
2. LAO CAI
3. HA GIANG
4. SON LA
5. YEN BAI
6. TUYEN QUANG
7. BAC CAN
8. CAO BANG
9. LANG SON
10. THAI NGUYEN
11. VINH PHUC
12. PHU THO
13. HA TAY
14. HANOI
15. HUNG YEN
16. BAC NINH
17. BAC GIANG
18. HAI DUONG
19. QUANG NINH
20. HOA BINH
21. HA NAM
22. HAIPHONG
23. THAI BINH
24. NAM DINH
25. NINH BINH
26. THANH HOA
27. NGHI AN
28. HA TINH
29. QUANG BINH
30. QUANG TRI
31. HUE
32. DA NANG
33. QUANG NAM
34. KON TUM
35. QUANG NGAI
36. GIA LAY
37. BIN DINH
38. PHU YEN
39. DAC LAC
40. KHANH HOA
41. LAM DONG
42. NINH THUAN
43. BINH THUAN
44. BINH PHUOC
45. DONG NAY
46. TAY NINH
47. BINH DUONG
48. LONG AN
49. SAIGON
50. VUNG TAU
51. AN GIANG
52. DONG THAP
53. TIEN GIANG
54. BEN TRE
55. KIEN GIANG
56. CAN THO
57. VINH LONG
58. TRA VINH
59. SOC TRANG
60. BAC LIEU
61. CA MAU

Vietnam

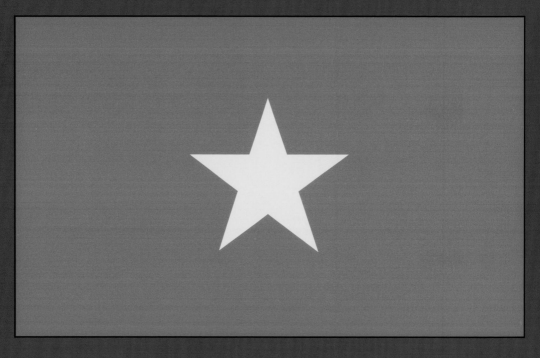

Foreign trade:

Imports—$79.37 billion: machinery and equipment, petroleum products, fertilizer, steel products, raw cotton, grain, cement, motorcycles

Exports—$63.73 billion: crude oil, marine products, fertilizer, steel products, raw cotton, rain, cement, motorcycles

Currency exchange rate: 17,481 Vietnamese dong = U.S. $1 (January 2009)

*GDP, or gross domestic product, is the total value of goods and services produced in a country annually (here estimated using the purchasing power parity method).

All figures are 2008 estimates unless otherwise noted.

Sources: CIA World Factbook, 2008; Bloomberg.com.

The People

Population: 86,116,560 (July 2008 est.)
Ethnic groups: Vietnamese 85%-90%, Chinese, Hmong, Thai, Khmer,

Cham, mountain groups

Age Structure:

    0–14 years: 25.6%

    15–64 years: 68.6%

    65 years and over: 5.8%

Population growth rate: 0.99% (2004 est.)

    Birth rate: 16.47 births/1,000 population (2004 est.)

    Infant mortality rate: 23.61 deaths/1,000 live births

    Death rate: 6.18 deaths/1,000 population

Life expectancy at birth:

    total population: 71.33 years

    males: 68.52 years

    females: 74.33 years

Total fertility rate: 1.86 children born/woman

Religions: Buddhist, Hoa Hao, Cao Dai, Christian (predominantly Roman Catholic, some Protestant), indigenous beliefs, Muslim

Languages: Vietnamese (official), English (increasingly favored as a second language), some French, Chinese, and Khmer; mountain area languages (Mon-Khmer and Malayo-Polynesian)

Literacy: 90.3% (2002 est.)

All figures are 2008 estimates unless otherwise indicated.

Source: CIA World Factbook, 2008.

Ahmed, Akbar S. *Islam Today*. London and New York: I.B. Tauris Publishers, 1999.

Boulnois, Luce. *Silk Road: Monks, Merchants and Warriors on the Silk Road*. Hong Kong: Odyssey Publications, 2004.

Esposito, John L. *Islam: The Straight Path*. 3rd ed. New York: Oxford University Press, 1998.

Esposito, John L. et al., eds. *Asian Islam in the 21st Century*. New York: Oxford University Press, 2008.

Gordon, Matthew S. *Islam*. New York: Oxford University Press, 2002.

Hildinger, Eric. *Warriors of the Steppe: A Military History of Central Asia*. New York: Da Capo Press, 2001.

Hourani, Albert. *A History of the Arab Peoples*. Cambridge, Mass.: The Belknap Press of Harvard University Press, 1991.

Lapidus, Ira M. *A History of Islamic Societies*. Cambridge, UK: Cambridge University Press, 1988.

Robinson, Neal. *Islam: A Concise Introduction*. Washington, D.C.: Georgetown University Press, 1999.

Roy, Olivier. *The New Central Asia: The Creation of Nations*. New York: New York University Press, 2000.

Saunders, J. J. *The History of the Mongol Conquests*. Philadelphia: University of Pennsylvania Press, 2001.

Internet Resources

http://www.lonelyplanet.com/asia

This website, operated by travel guide publisher Lonely Planet, provides links to informative pages about each of the Asian countries.

http://www.cia.gov/cia/publications/the-world-factbook/index.html

The CIA World Factbook provides current information about the countries of Asia. Individual countries can be selected using a pull-down menu.

http://www.eurasianet.org/

This comprehensive site offers news coverage and background information on the countries of Central Asia.

http://centralasianews.net/

Another good source of news on Central Asia.

http://silkroadproject.org/

This site contains excellent background information on the Silk Road.

http://www.usindo.org

The website of the United States-Indonesian Society provides current information about USINDO programs and publications, as well as useful links.

http://www.islamawareness.net/Asia/China

Overview about Muslims in China. Includes excellent maps.

Afghanistan, *12*, 19, 27, 34–37
Akayev, Askar, *71*
Almaty, Kazakhstan, 21–22
animism, 19, 53, 77
Ashgabat, Turkmenistan, 22
Azerbaijan, 22–23, 38–41

Baikonur complex (Kazakhstan), *67*
Baku, Azerbaijan, 22–23
Banda Aceh, Indonesia, 23
Bangladesh, 24, 42–45
Beslan, Russia, *89*
Bishkek, Kyrgyzstan, 23–24, *71*
Brunei, 46–49
Buddhism, 19, 49, *51*, 53, 57, 61, 65, 77, 85, 95, 99, 107, 119
Bukhara, Uzbekistan, 24
Burma, 50–53

China, 19, 27, 54–57
cities, 21–31
climate
    Afghanistan, 34
    Azerbaijan, 39
    Bangladesh, 42
    Brunei, 46
    Burma, 51
    China, 55
    India, 58
    Indonesia, 63
    Kazakhstan, 66
    Kyrgyzstan, 70

Malaysia, 75
Pakistan, 79
Philippines, 82
Russia, 88
Singapore, 92
Sri Lanka, 96
Tajikistan, 100
Thailand, 104
Turkmenistan, 108
Uzbekistan, 112
Vietnam, 116

Dhaka, Bangladesh, 24
Dushanbe, Tajikistan, 24–25

economy
    Afghanistan, *35*, 36–37
    Azerbaijan, 40–41
    Bangladesh, 44–45
    Brunei, 48–49
    Burma, 52–53
    China, 56–57
    India, 59–60
    Indonesia, 64–65
    Kazakhstan, 68–69
    Kyrgyzstan, 71–72
    Malaysia, 76–77
    Pakistan, 80–81
    Philippines, 82, 84
    Russia, 90
    Singapore, 93–94
    Sri Lanka, 96, 98
    Tajikistan, 102–103

Numbers in **bold italic** refer to captions.

Index

Thailand, 104, 106
Turkmenistan, 110
Uzbekistan, 114–115
Vietnam, 116–117
ethnic groups
Afghanistan, 37
Azerbaijan, 41
Bangladesh, 45
Brunei, 49
Burma, 53
China, 57
India, 61
Indonesia, 65
Kazakhstan, 69
Kyrgyzstan, 73
Malaysia, 77
Pakistan, 81
Philippines, 84
Russia, 91
Singapore, 95
Sri Lanka, 98
Tajikistan, 103
Thailand, 106
Turkmenistan, 111
Uzbekistan, 115
Vietnam, 118

five pillars of Islam, 16
     See also Islam
flags
Afghanistan, 36
Azerbaijan, 40
Bangladesh, 44
Brunei, 48
Burma, 52
China, 56–57

India, 60
Indonesia, 64
Kazakhstan, 68
Kyrgyzstan, 72
Malaysia, 76
Pakistan, 80
Philippines, 84
Russia, 88
Singapore, 94
Sri Lanka, 98
Tajikistan, 102
Thailand, 106
Turkmenistan, 110
Uzbekistan, 114
Vietnam, 118
Frunze. *See* Bishkek, Kyrgyzstan
fundamentalism (Islamic), 14
     See also Islam

Genghis Khan, 28
geographic features
Afghanistan, 34, 36
Azerbaijan, 38–39
Bangladesh, 42, 44
Brunei, 46
Burma, 50–51
China, 54–55
India, 58–59
Indonesia, 62–63
Kazakhstan, 66, 68
Kyrgyzstan, 70–71
Malaysia, 74–75
Pakistan, 78–79
Philippines, 82
Russia, 86–89
Singapore, 92–93

Sri Lanka, 96
Tajikistan, 100, 102
Thailand, 104
Turkmenistan, 108–109
Uzbekistan, 112, 114
Vietnam, 116
Great Mosque (Mecca), *17*

Hinduism, 19, 45, 61, 65, 81, 95,
  99, 107
Hughes, Chris, *12*

Icheri Sehir (Baku, Azerbaijan), 22
Id Kah Mosque (Kashgar, China),
  27
India, 19, 26–27, 58–59
Indonesia, 23, 25, 62–63
Islam
  five pillars of, 16
  founding and spread of, 13,
    15–19
  number of followers of, 14, *32*
Islamabad, Pakistan, 25

Jakarta, Indonesia, 25
Jammu and Kashmir, India, 26–27

Kabul, Afghanistan, 27
Kampong Ayer, Brunei, *47*
Karachi, Pakistan, *79*
Kashgar, China, 27
Kazakhstan, 21–22, 66–69
Kuala Lumpur, Malaysia, 28, *29*
Kukeldash Madrassa (Tashkent,
  Uzbekistan), *113*
Kyrgyz University, 24

Kyrgyzstan, 23–24, 70–73

languages
  Afghanistan, 37
  Azerbaijan, 41
  Brunei, 49
  Burma, 53
  China, 57
  India, 61
  Indonesia, 65
  Pakistan, 81
  Philippines, 85
  Russia, 91
  Singapore, 95
  Sri Lanka, 99
  Thailand, 107
  Turkmenistan, 111
  Uzbekistan, 115
  Vietnam, 119

Makhtumkuli, 22
Malaysia, 28, *29*, 74–77
maps
  Afghanistan, 34
  Azerbaijan, 38
  Bangladesh, 42
  Brunei, 46
  Burma, 50
  China, 54
  India, 58
  Indonesia, 62–63
  Kazakhstan, 66
  Kyrgyzstan, 70
  Malaysia, 74–75
  Pakistan, 78
  Philippines, 83

Index

Russia, 86–87
Singapore, 92
Sri Lanka, 97
Tajikistan, 100
Thailand, 105
Turkmenistan, 108
Uzbekistan, 112
Vietnam, 117
Martyrs' Monument (Shahid
    Minar), 24
Mecca, 15–16, *17*
Medina, 15–16
Middle East, 14–15, 16–17
Mongols, 28, 30
Mughal Empire, *20*, 27
Muhammad, 13, *14*, 15–16
    See also Islam
Multimedia Super Corridor (Kuala
    Lumpur, Malaysia), 28

natural resources
    Afghanistan, 36
    Azerbaijan, 40
    Bangladesh, 44
    Brunei, 48
    Burma, 52
    China, 56
    India, 59
    Indonesia, 64
    Kazakhstan, 68
    Kyrgyzstan, 72
    Malaysia, 76
    Pakistan, 80
    Philippines, 92
    Russia, 90
    Singapore, 93

Sri Lanka, 96
Tajikistan, 102
Thailand, 104
Turkmenistan, 110
Uzbekistan, 114
Vietnam, 116
Niu Jie Mosque (Beijing, China),
    55

Pakistan, 19, 25, 26–27, 78–81
Petronas Twin Towers (Kuala
    Lumpur, Malaysia), 28
Philippines, 82–85
Polo, Marco, 13
population
    Afghanistan, 37
    Azerbaijan, 41
    Bangladesh, 45
    Brunei, 49
    Burma, 53
    China, 57
    India, 61
    Indonesia, 65
    Kazakhstan, 69
    Kyrgyzstan, 73
    Malaysia, 77
    Pakistan, 81
    Philippines, 84
    Russia, 90
    Singapore, 95
    Sri Lanka, 98
    Tajikistan, 103
    Thailand, 106
    Turkmenistan, 111
    Uzbekistan, 115
    Vietnam, 118

See also cities

Qur'an, *14*, 15
    See also Islam

Registan (Samarkand, Uzbekistan),
    30
Russia, 86–91

Samarkand, Uzbekistan, 28, 30
Shah Faisal Mosque (Islamabad,
    Pakistan), 25
Silk Road, 19, 23, 24, 27, 28, 31
Singapore, 92–95
Sri Lanka, 96–99

Taj Mahal, *20*
Tajik Academy of Sciences, 25
Tajikistan, 24–25, 100–103

Tashkent, Uzbekistan, 30–31
Tashkent State Economic
    University, 31
Thailand, 104–107
Timur (Tamerlane), 28, 30, 31
Turkmenistan, 22, 108–111

United Nations Educational,
    Scientific and Cultural
    Organization (UNESCO), 24, 30
Uygurs (ethnic group), 27
    See also ethnic groups
Uzbekistan, 24, 28, 30–31,
    112–115

Vietnam, 116–119

Yathrib. *See* Medina
Yazdegerd III, 17

Picture Credits

The **FOREIGN POLICY RESEARCH INSTITUTE (FPRI)** served as editorial consultants for the MAJOR MUSLIM NATIONS series. FPRI is one of the nation's oldest "think tanks." The Institute's Middle East Program focuses on Gulf security, monitors the Arab-Israeli peace process, and sponsors an annual conference for teachers on the Middle East, plus periodic briefings on key developments in the region.

Among the FPRI's trustees is a former Secretary of State and a former Secretary of the Navy (and among the FPRI's former trustees and interns, two current Undersecretaries of Defense), not to mention two university presidents emeritus, a foundation president, and several active or retired corporate CEOs.

The scholars of FPRI include a former aide to three U.S. Secretaries of State, a Pulitzer Prize–winning historian, a former president of Swarthmore College and a Bancroft Prize–winning historian, and two former staff members of the National Security Council. And the FPRI counts among its extended network of scholars—especially its Inter-University Study Groups—representatives of diverse disciplines, including political science, history, economics, law, management, religion, sociology, and psychology.

DR. HARVEY SICHERMAN is president and director of the Foreign Policy Research Institute in Philadelphia, Pennsylvania. He has extensive experience in writing, research, and analysis of U.S. foreign and national security policy, both in government and out. He served as Special Assistant to Secretary of State Alexander M. Haig Jr. and as a member of the Policy Planning Staff of Secretary of State James A. Baker III. Dr. Sicherman was also a consultant to Secretary of the Navy John F. Lehman Jr. (1982–1987) and Secretary of State George Shultz (1988).

A graduate of the University of Scranton (B.S., History, 1966), Dr. Sicherman earned his Ph.D. at the University of Pennsylvania (Political Science, 1971), where he received a Salvatori Fellowship. He is author or editor of numerous books and articles, including *America the Vulnerable: Our Military Problems and How to Fix Them* (FPRI, 2002) and *Palestinian Autonomy, Self-Government and Peace* (Westview Press, 1993). He edits *Peacefacts*, an FPRI bulletin that monitors the Arab-Israeli peace process.

DOROTHY KAVANAUGH is a freelance writer who lives near Philadelphia. Her books include *Islam, Christianity, Judaism* (Mason Crest, 2004).